Searching For Happiness
SOME SUGGESTIONS ON HOW TO FIND IT

by Daniel H. King, Sr.

truth
BOOKS

www.truthbooks.net

Guardian of Truth Foundation
C E I Bookstore
220 S. Marion, St. • Athens, AL 35611
1-855-49BOOKS or 1-855-492-6657

ISBN 10: 1-58427-227-9

ISBN 13: 978-158427-227-4

truth
BOOKS

www.truthbooks.net

Guardian of Truth Foundation
C E I Bookstore
220 S. Marion, St. • Athens, AL 35611
1-855-49BOOKS or 1-855-492-6657

Table of Contents

Preface

As this manuscript was being finalized, the press announced the death of Anna Nicole Smith at age 39 at a South Florida hospital after she was discovered unconscious in her hotel room. This young woman was a reality TV star, Playboy Playmate of the year in 1993, ex-wife of octogenarian billionaire J. Howard Marshall II, and a former Guess jeans model. Her son Daniel, age 20, had died a year earlier under similar circumstances. Dr. Cyril Wecht who performed an autopsy of Daniel said that the young man died from a lethal combination of Zoloft, Lexapro and methadone. Regarding the death of Anna Nicole: "Undoubtedly it will be found at the end of the day that drugs featured in her death as they did in the death of poor Daniel," said a former attorney for Smith in the Bahamas, Michael Scott. Only a few months prior it had been discovered that she was taking methadone and "a rather high dose of Zanax during her pregnancy" in spite of the danger it posed to her unborn child. Autopsy blood tests showed that nine separate prescription drugs were present in her body at the time of death. Cause of death was due to a "combined drug intoxication," and thus "accidental overdose."

This is only the latest in an extremely long list of celebrities who have been seduced into the drug culture and have succumbed to its tragic results. Comedian and actor John Belushi at age 33, Tommy Bolin of Deep Purple at 25, John Bonham of Led Zeppelin at 32, Tony Caldwell of the Marshall Tucker Band, supermodel Gia Carangi, Gene Clark of the Byrds, Steve Clark of Def Leppard, Kurt Cobain of Nirvana at 27, actress Dorothy Dandridge at 42, Tommy Dorsey at 51, manager of the Beatles Brian Epstein at 32, comedian Chris Farley at 32, Andy Gibb of the Bee Gees, Tommy Hatfield of the Righteous Brothers, folk musician Tim Hardin, actress Margeuax Hemingway at 41, legendary guitarist Jimi Hendrix at 27, Gregory Herbet of Blood, Sweat & Tears, jazz singer Billie Holladay at 45, Howard Hughes at age 70, actress Anissa Jones who played Buffy on *Family Affair*, rock and roller Janis Joplin at age 27, John Kahn of the Jerry Garcia Band, David Kennedy, fourth child of politician Robert F. Kennedy, noted pianist Kenny Kirkland, Canadian hockey player John Kordic, American pornographic actress Arcadia Lake, French pornographic actress Karen Lancaume, actress Carole Landis, Rudy Lewis of the Drifters, fright film star Bela Lugosi, musician Pig Pen McKernan of the Grateful Dead, Robbie McIntosh of the Average White Band, actress Marilyn Monroe, Keith Moon of the Who, Jim Morrison of the Doors at 27, pornographic film star Dave Murray, Brent Mydland of the Grateful Dead, billionaire heiress Christina Onassis, actor Hugh O'Connor of *In the Heat of the Night*, Tour de France winner Marco Pantani, singer Esther Phillips, John Phillips of the Mamas and Papas, actor River Phoenix at 23, actress Dana Plato at 34, singer and film star Elvis Presley at 42, comic and actor Freddie Prinze at 22, musician Michael Rudetsky of Culture Club, David Ruffin of the Temptations, John Schermie of Three Dog Night, Bon Scott of AC/DC, baseball player Eric Show, film producer Don Simpson had 20 different drugs in his body at the time of his death, Hillel Slovak of the Red Hot Chile Peppers died at age 26 of a heroine overdose, comedian, writer and actor Eric Soto, 34-year-old Layne Staley of Alice in Chains, 26 year old pornographic actor Joey Stefano, actress Inger Stevens,

Vinnie Taylor of Sha Na Na, Gary Thain of Uriah Heep, playwright George Trakl, 34-year-old author D. M. Turner, three time winner of the World Series of Poker Stu Ungar at age 45, 21-year-old Sid Vicious of the Sex Pistols, female boxer and martial artist Shelby Walker at 31, country music singer Keith Whitley of alcohol poisoning, Dennis Wilson of the Beach Boys at 39, country music star Hank Williams died of drug and alcohol use, and beautiful Hollywood starlet Natalie Wood drowned while intoxicated.

This list goes on and on. I intentionally made it long in order to illustrate how many there are that appear on the full list. Even then I chose only about one name in ten, and all of them are the most recognizable to the average reader. Undoubtedly you can think of several we have not mentioned. Our point is that those whom we have listed achieved fame and fortune, and yet they were not at all happy. If they were, then why were they trying to drown their sorrows in drugs and alcohol? Why were they willing to risk their lives for a temporary comatose state, a cheap thrill, a momentary "rush," a drug or alcohol induced "high"? Obviously they were looking for something that their money could not buy them and their fame could not give them.

That "something" is called contentment or happiness. All of those listed above had achieved some considerable level of earthly success. None of the things they had achieved, however, was able to give them happiness. Notoriety could not do it. Possessions could not do it. Attainments could not deliver. Wealth has never been able to provide happiness. So, many of them were rich and famous—and completely miserable.

Hence, the reason for this short book. The rich and famous are not the only ones with a problem in this department. Many people of average means and quite normal abilities are struggling with identical difficulties. Most suffer in silence with little or no hope of deliverance. The blessed fact is that deliverance is easily within the reach of everyone.

At the heart of this material lies a sermon that I have preached in many churches over the better part of the last two decades. In October of 2006 it was delivered in Franklin, Kentucky at the 31W North congregation where my good friend Steve Monts is the preacher. One of the members there is Nancy Wright. She is a cancer survivor who heard it, said that she was greatly encouraged by it, and asked that I put it into print. When I ran into her at the Truth Bookstore in Bowling Green a few weeks later she inquired as to whether I had started it yet. I told her that I had not, but promised that I would soon. So, I went home that week and began work on it. I want to thank Nancy for her encouragement, and dedicate this effort to her and all others who courageously fight this dreadful disease. Among their number are my good friend Gary Finch and my sister-in-law Helen Chapman Zagata. I pray that all of them will win their battle with this silent but savage intruder and live to be "old and full of years."

The Universal Quest

The most pervasive search in human experience is the quest for happiness. No matter where you go in this world people are strenuously looking for it, whether consciously or unconsciously. They may not even know what to call it, or how to describe it, but they are after it. And usually they are hoping to find it somewhere else; wherever they are at the time, is not where it is to be found. Those in the frigid North Country frequently picture it somewhere on a south sea island. Some in the islands think it must be in the green hills of Kentucky. Hunters in the bluegrass state often picture it in the West where mule deer, elk, and buffalo still roam. Fishermen dream of the sky-blue salt waters of the ocean or of rolling mountain streams where trout and salmon are found in abundance. Golfers may think in terms of the "hidden links," the Old Course at St. Andrews in Scotland, the Ballyliffin Golf Club in Ireland, or even the St. Enodoc Golf Club in the southwest of England. City dwellers long for the quiet country life. Country folk pine for the shopping centers, conveniences, and fine restaurants of the big city.

Clearly it is an elusive prey. Many people will come right out and say, "I am not happy." If you ask them what would make them so, they may look back at you with a blank stare. Not only are they unhappy, they have no idea what it would take to make them happy. Seldom do you hear anyone say that they have achieved it. Occasionally someone will claim it, but not very often, and sometimes not for very long. It is a rare treasure. And it is fleeting. Frequently people will reveal through subtle hints that they are in pursuit of it. Occasionally they will come right out and say that they are looking for it. Interestingly, Nathaniel Hawthorne said, "Happiness is a butterfly, which, when pursued, is always just beyond your grasp, but which, if you will sit down quietly, may alight upon you."

People are universally striving after happiness, hunting and searching to find it. That much is certain. Remez Sasson insightfully said in his brief essay "The Happiness Factor":

If you analyze people's actions, you will come to the conclusion that they all seek happiness. Every act is in fact a search for it, even if on the surface it doesn't look so. Happiness is always the main target.

> "Happiness is a butterfly, which, when pursued, is always just beyond your grasp, but which, if you will sit down quietly, may alight upon you."
>
> — *Nathaniel Hawthorne*

_____

_____

_____

_____

_____

_____

_____

_____

_____

_____

Pursuit of anything in this world, without a healthy consideration of the ultimate and eternal consequences of our actions, leads only to frustration and emptiness.

_____

_____

_____

_____

_____

_____

_____

_____

_____

Going to the movies, eating in a restaurant or going to a party, are motivated by the desire to be happy. Sometimes the movie is not interesting, the food is not good and the party is boring. Then the search goes on. Maybe the next time the search will be more successful.

If the activity is pleasing, there might be a feeling of happiness, and then this activity is sought again in order to repeat this pleasant feeling.

Who does not dream of a vacation in some fascinating location, a new car, a new house, or the ideal match? All people daydream, and some even try to make their dreams a reality. And why is that? In order to be happy.

Aristotle in his *Ethics* is said to have written, "Happiness is the meaning and the purpose of life, the whole aim and end of human existence." One of the most significant statements in world history declares that men "are endowed by their Creator with certain inalienable rights; that among these are life, liberty, and the pursuit of happiness." These words, of course, are found in the *Declaration of Independence*. They are both insightful and incredibly profound. This is true because happiness is the goal that we all crave most, and the supreme object of our existence on this planet. Therefore, any mode of governing men that allows for the "pursuit of happiness" in a free and unencumbered way is bound to be popular and tremendously successful.

Solomon, the sage of ancient Israel, sought to find happiness in all of the places that people in every age have looked for it. He tried pleasure, wine and women, music and recreation, possessions, great construction projects, and even pursued higher learning (he called it "wisdom"). He remarked, "Whatsoever my eyes desired I kept not from them; I withheld not my heart from any joy; for my heart rejoiced because of all my labor; and this was my portion from all my labor. Then I looked on all the works that my hands had wrought, and on the labor that I had labored to do; and, behold, all was vanity and a striving after wind, and there was no profit under the sun" (Eccl. 2:10, 11). Pursuit of anything in this world, without a healthy consideration of the ultimate and eternal consequences of our actions, leads only to frustration and emptiness. It is the divine element that gives ultimate meaning to life in the physical world. At the last, he concluded man ought to, "Fear God, and keep his commandments; for this is the whole duty of man" (Eccl. 12:13). His point is, that in the pursuit of happiness man ought to keep his wits about him, control his wandering and unending appetites (6:9), and realize that in all of this searching there must be some recognition of the place of the Maker in the picture. He must be answered to at some point (12:14), so individual happiness should not be viewed as an end in itself.

No grander theme ever engaged the powers of burning eloquence or inspired poetic fire. Myriads of Muses and Masters throughout the centuries have sung its praises. Alexander Pope, for example, opined as follows:

O happiness! Our being's end and aim!

Good, pleasure, ease, content! Whate'er thy name:

That something still which prompts eternal sigh,

For which we bear to live, or dare to die.

A simple look at modern advertising shows the human creature's insatiable longing for happiness. The gist of the wording reveals at the core of almost every one of these popular phrases the essence of the quest: "Live it up!" "Get more out of life!" "Go for the gusto!" "Have more fun!" On and on we could go with this. There can be no argument against it. You know that it is so. In point of fact, it is more revealing of our inner selves than we might like to admit. Advertisers are professionals, and they know what we are all looking for. So it is to those inner longings that their commercials inevitably and incessantly speak! Moreover, we observe even in the fanatical exploitation of pleasure the presence of this pursuit of happiness. Abuse of alcohol, drugs, and even sex, are all clear indications that the soul of man is looking for something. And more often than not, the resultant misery and pain that grow out of such abuse demonstrate that he is not finding what he is searching so intently and doggedly for.

Some sort of proper definition would probably be helpful at this juncture. What is happiness? Dr. Maxwell Maltz, in his book Five Minutes to Happiness defines it as, "A state of mind or habit where we have pleasant thoughts the greater part of the time." We either have this state of mind or we don't. And if we do not, then our thoughts are troubled and we are certainly looking about for it. It is especially interesting to note that many people who seem to have all of the things that so many other people dream about and hope for, are not at all happy. This reminds us of the advice given by La Rochefoucauld: "Before we set our hearts too much upon any thing, let us examine how happy those are who already possess it." Fortune, fame, leisure, possessions—each one of these has been tried by others and they have come up short. The Hollywood elite illustrate their dissatisfaction with the fashionable accessories of luxurious living daily. Their lives are empty and cold in spite of the fact that they are rich and famous. Perhaps Juvenal was right when he observed, "Luxury is more deadly than any foe." Pierre Bezúkhov in Tolstoy's War and Peace learned this lesson, during his period of captivity, namely that "man is created for happiness; that happiness lies in himself, in the sat-

Abuse of alcohol, drugs, and even sex, are all clear indications that the soul of man is looking for something.

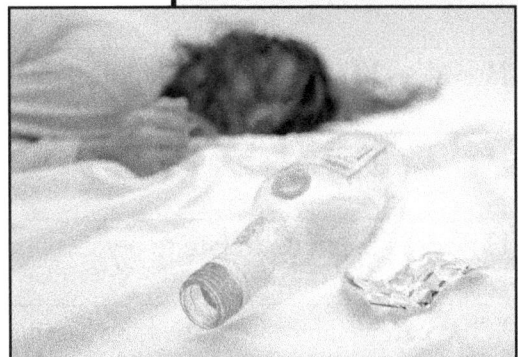

isfaction of his natural human cravings; that all unhappiness arises not from privation but from superfluity." How else can we explain these common characteristics of the privileged class—their many divorces, outrageous behavior, strange political quirks, odd religious and philosophical notions, outright criminality, their many suicides or their suicidal drug binges? Certainly this is not the stuff of which happiness is made!

At the same time, there seem to be a few people out there who have very little of what others consider necessary for happiness, and yet they seem blissfully happy. How ironic this appears on the surface, and yet so very perfectly an illustration of the point we are trying to make in the present essay: The pursuit of happiness is not an easy or simple quest. With so many looking in all of the wrong places, it might be wise to figure out in advance where the "happy hunting ground" may be found and what it might look like before we expend too much energy on a fruitless trail that leads nowhere.

Someone has explained that, "Happiness and trouble stand at everyone's gate. Yours is the choice which one you will let in." Lots of folks, by their unfortunate misunderstanding of how to be happy have let this other fellow through the gate. In the lines that follow, we hope at the very least to point you in the direction of this "happy hunting ground" so that you will not let the wrong visitor through your gate.

Questions

1. Provide a working definition of "happiness": _____

_____

2. How does happiness relate to attainments? _____

_____

3. How does happiness relate to notoriety? _____

_____

4. How does happiness relate to wealth? _____

_____

5. How does happiness relate to possessions? _____

_____

6. What can we learn from the long list of suicides, drug and alcohol abuse cases, disastrous marriages and multiple divorces among Hollywood personalities, famous entertainers, accomplished athletes, eminent writers, noted instrumentalists and vocalists? _____

_____

7. Pick out one person from the lengthy list of personalities in the Preface whom you have particular interest in, and tell the class something about this person and his particular situation. What lessons can we draw from this wasted life? _____

_____

8. Geographically speaking, where is happiness to be found? Is the answer to this question different for different people? Illustrate how this is true or untrue. _____

_____

9. Discuss Nathaniel Hawthorne's statement that "happiness is a butterfly, which, when pursued, is just beyond your grasp, but which, if you will sit down quietly, may alight upon you." If this is so, how does it help us in our own personal "pursuit of happiness"? _____

10. The American *Declaration of Independence* says that men are, "endowed by their Creator with certain inalienable rights; that among these are life, liberty and the pursuit of happiness." Discuss this profound statement in the context of the modern thinking which seems to intimate that everyone in America is somehow guaranteed happiness as their birthright. Is this really what the Founders of our great nation intended by these words? _____

11. King Solomon, the most likely writer of the book of Ecclesiastes, experimented with all sorts of things in his search for contentment (Eccl. 2:1-26). Read the entirety of this passage together in class. In the end, you will notice that he came up empty in his search among the various pleasurable enterprises in this world (2:11, 17, 18, 22-23, 26). What is the lesson for us in Solomon's search? _____

12. At the conclusion of the book, Ecclesiastes says, "Fear God, and keep his commandments, for this is the whole duty of man" (12:13). How does God fit into this picture of a man "searching for happiness"? _____

13. How does modern advertising reflect the inner search for meaning and joy in life? _____

14. Does advertising at times create a false sense of where true happiness may be found? Provide a few illustrations of this from your own experience with advertisers on TV, in magazines, etc. _____

15. "Before we set our hearts too much upon any thing, let us examine how happy those are who already possess it." How true is this? If you think it is, or is not, show by at least two examples why you have come to the conclusion that you have. _____

16. In the novel *War and Peace*, one of Tolstoy's characters reflects that "all unhappiness arises not from privation but from superfluity." Is this true? If so, it may suggest that the poor are generally happier than the rich! In your own experience, can you think of people who were poor but seemed blissfully happy? How about people who were rich but appeared to be miserable? _____

Jesus Came to Bring True Happiness

> . . . Christ saw as part of his mission among the sons and daughters of men to present to the human mind certain specific principles which, if learned and observed, would lead to the enjoyment of happiness.

Given the almost universal nature of this search for contentment, is there any wonder, therefore, that Jesus Christ placed such an emphasis upon happiness in conjunction with a relationship with God in the opening lines of his Mountaintop Sermon recorded in Matthew 5-7? In his own words,

> Blessed are the poor in spirit: for theirs is the kingdom of heaven. Blessed are those who mourn: for they shall be comforted. Blessed are the meek: for they shall inherit the earth. Blessed are those who hunger and thirst after righteousness: for they shall be filled. Blessed are the merciful: for they shall obtain mercy. Blessed are the pure in heart: for they shall see God. Blessed are the peacemakers: for they shall be called the children of God. Blessed are those who are persecuted for righteousness' sake: for theirs is the kingdom of heaven. Blessed are you, when men shall revile you, and persecute you, and shall say all manner of evil against you falsely, for my sake. Rejoice, and be exceeding glad: for great is your reward in heaven: for so they persecuted the prophets who were before you (Matt. 5:3-12).

In these introductory words of the Sermon on the Mount, we discover manifest evidence that Jesus saw himself as the harbinger of the hidden secrets of true happiness. The Greek word that is so frequently used in that prologue to the Sermon is the meaningful term *makarios*. Jesus used it nine times in this section of the message he delivered there on that hill above the Sea of Galilee. It means "blessed, happy, to be congratulated." These beautiful beatitudes (from the Latin word *beatitudo*, "happiness" or "blessedness") are the most potent evidence found anywhere that Christ saw as part of his mission among the sons and daughters of men to present to the human mind certain specific principles which, if learned and observed, would lead to the enjoyment of happiness.

The angelic announcement at the birth of Jesus gave some hint of this aspect of the work of Christ as well. Luke's record of it reads thus:

> And the angel said to them, "Be not afraid; for behold, I bring you good tidings of great joy, which shall be to all the people: For there is born to you this day in the city of David a Savior, who is Christ the Lord" (Luke 2:10, 11).

Jesus said to his disciples as they waited in nervous anticipation on the night of his agonizing prayers in Gethsemane, betrayal and trial,

"Let not your heart be troubled, you believe in God, believe also in me" (John 14:1). He did not want them to suffer the same agonies that he was about to experience. That burden was his to bear, not theirs.

A funny story that well illustrates this point was told by Howard Jones of the Billy Graham Evangelistic Association. He related that on a certain occasion he was preaching from this verse to a remote tribe in the Sudan. He noticed that his interpreter was having some difficulty with this particular text, and after the service inquired about it. "Well," said the interpreter, "in the Sudanese language, the heart is not the seat of the emotions; the liver is. So when I translated your words, it came out, "Don't let your liver quiver!"

Christians have sometimes failed to see this side of God's character. In past ages, especially, some have viewed God differently than we do today. Instead of emphasizing the loving aspect of God, they saw only the judicial and punitive side of him. While it would be unfair to block out God's justice and wrath as though they do not exist in his nature, it would also be uncritical to fail to appreciate his grace and love as revealed to us in the person and work of Jesus Christ. God has shown us that he is a loving and forgiving Father waiting patiently for his prodigal children to return to him (Luke 15:20).

On a personal level, this point was brought home to me in the story of Sir James Young Simpson (1811-1870), a surgeon who practiced medicine in Scotland. It is difficult for us to imagine what it must have been like to operate on a patient in the days before anesthesia. Physicians worked with scalpel and saw upon patients strapped down, at times screaming in wretched agony. Every slice and turn of the knife or saw upon flesh and bone brought unimaginable pain to the pitiful subject of the operation. Dr. Simpson dreamed of finding a way of putting patients to sleep during surgery. On Monday evenings he periodically invited small groups of doctors to his home to experiment with various chemical agents. The physicians breathed in the vapors of the different chemicals as they burned over a brazier. Nothing worked until November 4, 1847. When they tried a crystal called chloroform, the doctors sniffed it and fell asleep. At last, he had his answer. However, he quickly ran into another problem. Some Christians argued that pain was a God-ordained part of life, and that it was immoral to relieve it this side of heaven. Simpson, being a good Bible student himself, quickly pointed out to them that God had put Adam to sleep when he performed surgery to remove his rib (see Gen. 2:21). His critics were silenced, and a new day dawned in medical science. An operating room was no longer a torture chamber. The lesson that we can draw from this is that God does not want his children to suffer. He

NOTES:

did not want Adam to suffer, and he does not want you to suffer. He wants you to be happy.

G. K. Chesterton said, "Joy is the gigantic secret of the Christian." Because we believe that Jesus was God in the flesh, we also know that understanding him and his words of advice for us present to our minds the truest and best secrets to happiness. It is our intent, therefore, in this brief treatise to underscore some of the abiding principles which lead to the enjoyment of happiness as they are taught in the Sermon on the Mount and elsewhere in Scripture. Take careful note of them, for if you ignore them enjoyment of life will in fact be all but impossible. Know and observe them, and whatever else may be said of your station in life or any other aspect of your existence, happiness will attend your every step.

Questions

1. Define the word "blessed" as Jesus used it in Matthew 5:3-12. What does it have to do with our search for happiness? _____

_____

2. What did the angelic announcement delivered at the time of the birth of Jesus into the world suggest about the nature of the Lord's task among men? _____

_____

3. How did the words "let not your hearts be troubled" lend encouragement to the bewildered disciples on the night of his betrayal? How ought they to provide consolation and solace to God's people today? _____

_____

4. Discuss the importance of a proper understanding of the balance in the nature of God between his mercy and his judgment, his benevolence and his wrath in terms of Romans 11:17-24? At different times in the history of the church has there been a tendency to accentuate one or the other? Where are we today? Is the balance perfect, slightly out of balance, or completely "off the chart"? _____

_____

_____

5. Does God have a desire to see his children suffer? Discuss this question in the light of the story of Sir James Young Simpson and the discovery of anesthesia. How does the narrative of woman's creation, recorded in Genesis 2:21, shed light upon this issue? _____

_____

_____

6. Read John 1:1-5; and later on in the same context, note especially v. 14. Read together Philippians 2:5-11 also. Both of these passages of Scripture emphasize the "enfleshment" or incarnation of God in Christ. They beautifully express the profound truth that God took upon himself a human body in order to redeem the fallen race from its sin. (Note also the words of the hymn: "Out of the ivory palaces, into a world of woe. Only his great eternal love, made my Savior go.") What is the great ultimate lesson of this with respect to God's desire to see the eternal happiness of his people? If "actions speak louder than words" then what do God's actions say to us? _____

_____

_____

Make Up Your Mind To Be Happy

> ## "Most people are just about as happy as they make up their minds to be."
>
> ### — Abraham Lincoln

Happiness is not achievable for some people because in their heart of hearts they prefer misery. Some people thrive on pain. Now, we understand that this sounds counterintuitive, but it is true nonetheless. Holy Scripture provides ample evidence of this strange and curious fact, and so does common experience. Abraham Lincoln once said, "Most people are just about as happy as they make up their minds to be."

This suggests that in large measure those who are miserable and sink into the dark pit of depression have somehow determined that it is their preference to be there. In our own experience, we have seen many cases which demonstrate the truth of this weighty observation. Now, this does not imply that they have *consciously* made this choice. It may well be that they have chosen this route unconsciously or even subconsciously, or that they simply do not know any better than to head off in the direction they are going. But the end result is the same. They are miserable, and they are wallowing in the black muck of that misery in spite of the fact that there is another and superior way. So, in a very real sense, *they have chosen misery over happiness!*

A fellow once asked a lady who was singing happily as she hung out her clothes to dry on the line in her yard: "Where did you find all of that happiness?" The questioner could not possibly see himself merrily engaged in this menial chore. "I did not find it," she replied, "I made it." Far too many of us think that it is somehow possible to find happiness, or we may buy it, create it, or synthetically induce it. In fact, none of these methods will bring it about. Agnes Repplier said, "It is not easy to find happiness in ourselves, and it is not possible to find it elsewhere." If we do not find it somewhere within the deepest recesses of our own souls, then we will never find it. It is not possible to find it elsewhere. The potential for its enjoyment is there, hidden within each one of us, waiting patiently for the moment of discovery.

Happiness is a state of mind that is self-induced. If that were not so, the words of Christ would not make any sense at all in the context of persecution and mistreatment by others. Said the Lord, "Blessed are those who are persecuted for righteousness' sake: for theirs is the kingdom of heaven. Blessed are you, when men shall revile you, and persecute you, and shall say all manner of evil against you falsely, for my sake. Rejoice, and be exceeding glad: for great is your reward in heaven: for so they persecuted the prophets who were before you" (Matt. 5:10-12).

It becomes clear from this that happiness is a state of mind that is attainable in every conceivable circumstance. Not easily so, in some instances, but it is reachable. We see it in the lives and examples of the apostles when they were later persecuted for their faith: "They therefore departed from the presence of the council, rejoicing that they were counted worthy to suffer dishonor for the Name" (Acts 5:41). These men had barely escaped this confrontation with their lives; the council at first had sought to kill them, but cooler heads prevailed, and in the end they were only beaten and warned of worse things to come. Instead of worrying about what might happen in the future, or else concentrating upon the considerable pain that had been inflicted upon their persons, they rejoiced that they had been counted worthy to suffer this dishonor for the Lord's name. It is evident that in their case, at least, they had made up their minds to be happy in spite of these rather dire circumstances.

Perhaps in this case happiness ought to be rendered as "serenity," for it certainly implies the acceptance of unpleasant surroundings or circumstances that for many people would have been more consistent with misery than of happiness. Reinhold Niebuhr (1892-1971), Professor of Practical Theology at Union Theological Seminary, was the original author of the so-called "Serenity Prayer" which has come to be used by Alcoholics Anonymous, Narcotics Anonymous, and other Twelve Step programs. Niebuhr wrote it for a sermon in about 1932. The original version read as follows: "O God and Heavenly Father, Grant to us the serenity of mind to accept that which cannot be changed; the courage to change that which can be changed, and the wisdom to know the one from the other, through Jesus Christ our Lord, Amen." In its modern version, many of the religious aspects of its origin are stripped away: "God grant me the serenity to accept the things I cannot change, courage to change the things I can, and the wisdom to know the difference." This is characteristic of modernity. It strips away religion from life, and then wonders why things do not continue to function properly. This is like removing the wheels from a car and wondering why it will not move. Man is a religious being, incurably religious, whether we like it or not. Augustine said, "You made us for yourself, and our heart is restless, until it reposes in you." Human beings are not suited to a happy existence without God. The great historian Will Durant wrote: "The greatest question of our time is not communism vs. individualism, nor Europe vs. America, not even the East vs. the West; it is whether men can bear to live without God."

"You made us for yourself, and our heart is restless, until it reposes in you."

— Augustine

Make Up Your Mind To Be Happy

17

> **Joy comes from within, and if we are robbed of it, this can only be by our own permission.**

True serenity is a uniquely Christian phenomenon. This is not to say that other religious traditions do not place emphasis upon it, for some do. But as a simple matter of history, what other religion can boast a record of thousands who gladly, even cheerfully, died for their faith under the iron hand of persecuting emperors and tyrants? Christianity is in a class all by itself.

James noted that the Christian ought to be happy when temptations come his way (Jas. 1:2, 12). "Count it all joy, my brethren," he said. In Paul's letter to the Philippians, written while he was in shackles at Rome (1:13), he attempted to cheer up his friends with the knowledge that God had used his unfortunate circumstance to reach even the Praetorian Guard with the gospel of Christ (1:12, 13). He used the word "joy" in this epistle constantly, urging them to rejoice with him at the success he had in proclaiming the message of the Savior (1:3, 4; 2:2; 3:1; 4:4). More important even than this, is his own explanation of his ability to rejoice in such frightening conditions: "I have learned in whatsoever state I am, therein to be content" (4:11).

So, according to Paul, this is learned behavior. One can learn to react to unfortunate and even disturbing circumstances in joy. This can only be so if happiness ultimately comes from within one's own heart. External conditions may temporarily effect our perception of it, but they cannot take it away unless we surrender it. Joy comes from within, and if we are robbed of it, this can only be by our own permission.

Christ came to give his people abundant life. He said, "I came that they may have life, and may have it abundantly" (John 10:10). If we do not enjoy abundant life, it is not because it is not available to us. We may waste away because of our own neglect of the plentiful nourishment that lies easily within reach of us in the soul's cupboard, but that cannot be blamed upon any but ourselves. The cupboard is full to overflowing. Joy is there for the taking.

Questions

1. Discuss the proposition, "Some people are not happy, because deep down they really prefer misery." Is this really possible? Is this mentality conscious or unconscious? _____

_____

2. Is it really accurate to say, "Happiness is a state of mind that is self-induced"? Are there external forces at work also? If so, what are some of them? _____

_____

3. Read Matthew 5:10-12. How does this passage shed light upon the issue? Is it really possible to be happy in the midst of pain or persecution? _____

_____

_____

4. In Acts 5:41 why did the disciples rejoice? Is there a difference in the "joy" described here and the joy one experiences at the birth of a new baby, or at the wedding of one of your children or grand-children? If so, what makes the difference? _____

_____

5. Is a state of true inner serenity a uniquely Christian phenomenon? How would you illustrate or demonstrate the validity of your answer? _____

_____

6. How may a Christian be happy during a season of temptation (see James 1:2, 12)? _____

_____

7. Paul said that he had learned the secret of contentment in every situation (Phil. 4:11). He urged the church at Philippi to rejoice with him in spite of his imprisonment (1:3-4, 12-13; 2:2; 3:1; 4:4)? How is this sort of contentment possible? It seems illogical, does it not? _____

_____

8. "If we are robbed of our joy, it must be by our permission that it is taken away." How would you evaluate this statement? Why would we willingly surrender it? _____

_____

Make Sure Your Thoughts Are Happy Ones

> **A happy person is not a person in a certain set of circumstances, but rather a person with a certain set of attitudes."**
>
> *— Hugh Downs*

"No man is happy unless he believes he is," wrote Publilius Syrus (100 B.C.) in his *Maxims*. This assuredly explains the strange phenomenon that so many of us have so often seen, namely, people who have every reason we can think of to be happy—and yet they are not. The Bible says, "As a man thinketh in his heart, so is he" (Prov. 23:7). Just as "we are what we eat," we also are what we think about all of the time. If we think happy thoughts, then we will be happy. On the other hand, if our thoughts are moribund and sad because we spend too much time thinking about gloomy and distressing events, or choose to fraternize regularly with cheerless and disconsolate people, then we will not be happy. We will become what we think about all the time, so we need to be careful about the content of our thoughts.

Hugh Downs once said, "A happy person is not a person in a certain set of circumstances, but rather a person with a certain set of attitudes." If we think sorrowful, distressful, painful, dark, and joyless thoughts, then we will be all of these undesirable attitudes wrapped up in a human personality. Most of us have met one or more of such folk, and they are not pleasant to be around. There is a very sad line that falls from the lips of Woody Allen's character in the movie *Annie Hall*: "Life can be divided into the horrible and miserable." Such folk do not make particularly agreeable companions.

A number of years ago there was a lady in the church where I worked as minister. She was very wealthy but utterly joyless. My wife and I visited with her often because we felt that she needed our encouragement. Her husband had died tragically a number of years before, and she was left bitter by the terrible news coverage which painted him as a man of questionable moral practices, when in reality he was a man of the highest and finest character. Speculation circulated as to the circumstances of his disappearance until his body was eventually found in the wilderness and it was determined that he had perished in a plane accident many days before. On one particular occasion, she informed us that she was very distressed because she had sold an automobile dealership a few years before and the new owner had been forced to return the asset to her in spite of the fact that she had been paid a substantial down payment and had received about two years of monthly payments. She said that she was very depressed at having to take care of this burdensome responsibility. I said to her teasingly, "Are you telling me that you were given a very substantial down payment, have received a number of months of large monthly payments, and now the entire thing has come back for you to sell it again? And you are unhappy, about what? Listen, I have a plan: Just sign the whole thing over to me, and I will bear the awful burden of it!" At that point, she smiled. Things were not nearly as bad as she had been making them out to be. This was in fact a dark cloud with a very silver lining. Within a few months she had resold the dealership, once more with a large down payment, and was comfortably receiving the monthly installments on a regular basis. She had made out like a bandit!

Her problem: She allowed herself to obsess over every misfortune— even over some things that were really not bad at all—and failed to consider all of the happy things in her life. While others were worried about making the house payment, being able to pay their taxes, concerned about large hospital bills not covered by insurance, or even having the wherewithal to provide groceries to feed a big family—she was unhappy because she had to deal with the hassle of selling a multi-million dollar property. Most of us would quite readily exchange places with her!

The patriarch Job cried out early in his dreadful experience with grief and pain, "What I most feared has befallen me, what I dreaded has overtaken me" (Job 3:25). The things we fear and dread the most very often overtake us. Several years back I dealt with a client in my work as a financial advisor who informed me early on in our relationship that all of her family was short-lived. She said that she did not expect to live to be old. I remember feeling very sad that she had this view of things, and tried to encourage her not to view things so negatively. She was in her early fifties. About four years later I received a call from one of the family members informing me that she was in the hospital dying of cancer. Immediately I began preparing the paperwork for the distribution of her estate. She died a few short days later. Perhaps a genetic predisposition was responsible for her premature death. There may have been environmental factors present. Perhaps lifestyle issues were at fault. Who knows? But, one thing I do know: the thing that she most feared had befallen her, what she had dreaded had overtaken her. All of us have known people who have thought the very worst of things would be coming upon them, only to see those ugly possibilities realized in real-life experiences months or even years later.

God does not want us to live in the shadow of the darkest evils. He would have us to live in light and joy. Through Isaiah the prophet, he spoke to his downcast people and said, "Say to them that are of a fearful heart, 'Be strong, fear not'" (Isa. 35:4). Is it not encouraging to

NOTES:

Fill up your mind with good things, wholesome things, virtuous things, happy things; there will be no room left for immorality or evil, sadness or depression.

know that the same power is available to help us optimistically imagine the best and finest things and perhaps by that means take the steps necessary to bring them about? In fact they are too often employed to bring about a negative result.

Always expect to be happy. Many of our hopes and dreams tend to be self-fulfilling. This is so because, often unconsciously, we take steps toward their fulfillment. After twenty years of intense research into what made super successful people tick, Napoleon Hill wrote: "Our brains become magnetized with the dominating thoughts which we hold in our minds, and by means of which no man is familiar, these magnets attract to us the forces, the people, and the circumstances of life which harmonize with the nature of our dominating thoughts." Of course, there are practical limits to this sort of thing, and he may have overstated his case somewhat, but there is certainly some truth to Hill's theory.

Our minds do tend to center upon certain dominating thoughts and thereby we set in motion a series of other thoughts and actions which will inevitably move us in the direction of our most immediate goal. If happiness is that goal, then that is where we will likely end up. In a sense it becomes a sort of self-fulfilling prophecy. Unfortunately, unhappiness is also a self-fulfilling prophecy. If we think upon the dark side of life too much, morbid thoughts will dominate and we will make ourselves miserable.

I remember visiting with a friend several years ago (ca. 1982) who was very clearly in a state of despondency. When I inquired about his cheerless state of mind, he explained it this way: "A couple of weeks ago I went to see the movie *The World According to Garp*. Since I saw it, I have been in a state of depression, and I cannot seem to come out of it." I told him that he had left me utterly speechless. "You mean to tell me, that here you are with a wonderful wife, a pleasant marriage, a beautiful home, a successful business—and yet you are depressed over a ridiculous movie produced by a bunch of Hollywood idiots! You have food to eat, clothing to wear, a nice house to live in, and someone warm to snuggle close to at night—and Hollywood has convinced you to be depressed! Have you lost your mind?"

In 1995 Nicolas Cage and Elisabeth Shue starred in the movie *Leaving Las Vegas*. This Hollywood production told the story of John O'Brien, a novelist and suicidal alcoholic who had a relationship with a prostitute in Las Vegas. Two weeks after the production of the film began, O'Brien killed himself. It was completed as a memorial to his sad and pitiful life. The film was highly praised and won critical acclaim. Cage won the Academy Award for Best actor and Shue was also nominated for Best Actress. In addition, the movie received nominations for Best Original

Screenplay and Best Director (Mike Figgis). I remember watching a very favorable review of the movie on television by a well-known reviewer that summarized the story-line of the film and praised almost every aspect of it. I thought to myself at the time: "What a downer! Who would want to go and purposely subject his mind to such trash! What possible 'redeeming value' can it have?" To this day I have never seen the movie, and have no intention of ever seeing it. For several years afterward I would not see a Nicolas Cage film because he had played the starring role in such a sad caricature of human life. Why must Hollywood focus so intently upon the sordid side of life? Who cares about how well it is written or acted if the story that it tells is this depressing? How can anyone fill his mind with such rubbish and come away from the experience the better for it?

As Paul closed out his letter to the Philippians, he encouraged them to fill their minds with positive things. He wrote: "Finally, brethren, whatever is true, whatever is honorable, whatever is just, whatever is pure, whatever is lovely, whatever is of good report; if there be any virtue, and if there be any praise, think on these things" (4:8, 9). The theory behind his logic is simple but profound. A gardener plants grass seed in a yard thickly, covering the space completely, leaving no bare spots. This is his intention. Weeds will inevitably intrude into the yard through the bare spots. If the lawn is covered, thick with grass, there is no room for weeds to proliferate. There is no place for them. That is the idea Paul was promoting. Fill up your mind with good things, wholesome things, virtuous things, happy things; there will be no room left for immorality or evil, sadness or depression.

Reject every opportunity to be miserable. Turn it down flat. Refuse to watch depressing movies or listen to music that brings the spirit low. There is so much in this world that is beautiful and exquisite, wholesome and healthy, pleasant and good that it is pointless to concentrate on such things. Why would we spend our hard-earned money to pay to watch or listen to them? This is like intentionally climbing onto a torturer's rack to see how the experience will turn out. Why subject yourself to the agony?

Think happy thoughts and expect always to be happy. Point your expectations in the direction of happiness, and nine times out of ten they will take you where you want to go.

NOTES:

1. "No man is happy unless he believes he is." This wise saying captures a truth which far too few appreciate. What can one do to convince himself/herself of the blessedness of his or her own estate? What method of reasoning should be used? _____

    _____

2. "We are what we think about all of the time." The importance of this recognition cannot be downplayed. If this is true, what can we do to reach the goal of greater happiness and contentment?

    _____

    _____

3. Hugh Downs is quoted as having said, "A happy person is not a person in a certain set of circumstances, but rather a person with a certain set of attitudes." What attitudes would you associate with realizing some sense of contentedness? _____

    _____

4. "Always expect to be happy. Many of our hopes and dreams are self-fulfilling." Do you agree with this analysis? Can you provide illustrations to show either that it is true or not true? _____

    _____

5. In Job 3:25 the patriarch said, "What I most feared has befallen me, what I dreaded has overtaken me." What are some of the most common "fears" and "dreads" of folks whom you know? How have those fears affected their mental state? If they were to change their way of thinking, or even obsessing, over such things, do you think they might perhaps be happier people? _____

    _____

6. Discuss Isaiah 35:4 in light of the question whether God wants his people to live in fear or not. Look at the following texts also: Gen. 15:1; 26:24; Exod. 14:13; 20:20; Deut. 1:21; 31:6, 8; Josh. 8:1; 2 Kings 6:16; Pss. 27:3; 46:2; 56:4; 118:6; Matt. 10:28, 31; 2 Tim. 1:7; Heb. 13:6; 1 John 4:18. _____

    _____

7. Hollywood has a tendency to concentrate on the most sordid aspects of human existence. Why is this so? Is a steady diet of Hollywood's productions healthy for the soul? Aside from the vulgarity, profanity and incessant sexuality, how do you think TV and the "big screen" movies unconsciously affect the thinking of people? _____

    _____

8. What is the most important lesson of Paul's admonition in Philippians 4:8, 9? How can we obey the requirements of this passage? What kinds of things would probably prove to be spiritually unhealthy for us, based on what Paul tells us in this text? _____

    _____

    _____

    _____

Count Your Blessings and Be Thankful

A Christian farmer was spending the day in a large city. Entering a restaurant for his noon meal, he found a table near a spirited group of young men. When his meal was served to him a few minutes later, he removed his hat, quietly bowed his head, and gave thanks for the food before him. One of the young fellows, observing his quiet moment of reverence, thought he would ridicule and embarrass the old gentleman. In a loud voice he asked, "Hey, farmer, does everyone do that where you live?" Without missing a beat, the old man glared at the callow youth and calmly replied, "No, son, the pigs don't."

Gratitude is not much appreciated these days. It is one of the fine virtues that has diminished with the coarsening of modern Western society. But there is an implicit affiliation that needs to be understood here, but is seldom appreciated. Thankful people tend also to be happy people. Those who have no sense of gratitude, on the other hand, tend not to be happy. There is an infallible logic to this; do not miss it. If you are grateful, then it is evident that you feel that you have something to be grateful for. Therefore, gratitude and happiness go hand in hand.

In the 1719 novel by Daniel Defoe, when Robinson Crusoe was shipwrecked on the lonely island that became his home for some twenty-eight years, he performed a sort of inventory of his assets and liabilities. He called these things "the evil and the good." He acknowledged that he had been cast on a desolate island, but that he was still alive—not drowned, as his ship's company had been. He was apart from human society, but he was not starving. He had no clothes, but he was in a hot climate where he did not have need for warm clothing. He was without means of self-defense, but he saw no wild beasts such as he had observed on the coast of Africa. He had no one to whom he could speak, but God had sent the ship so near to the shore that he could get out of it all the things necessary for his basic wants. So he concluded that there was not any condition in the world so miserable but that one could find something for which to be grateful. If we could, every one of us, learn to take such an inventory of our life, we would find the same thing to be true. There are always many reasons to be thankful. We just have to look for them.

> Even the things that seem bad at the time can prove to be blessings in disguise.

> Thankful people tend also to be happy people.

> "It is he who is always thankful to God, who wills everything that God willeth, who receives everything as an instance of God's goodness, and has a heart always ready to praise God for it."
>
> — *William Law*

Matthew Henry (1662-1714), the famous Bible scholar and commentator, was once accosted by thieves and robbed of his purse. This was an important event in his life because he was a relatively poor man. Nevertheless, these are the words that he wrote afterward in his diary regarding this painful experience:

> Let me be thankful first because I was never robbed before; second, although they took my purse, they did not take my life; third, because although they took my all, it was not much; and fourth, because it was I who was robbed, and not someone else.

Truly Henry displayed in these telling words what we might describe as "an attitude of gratitude." Very few people would be capable in such trying circumstances of seeing the positive side of this encounter with the ugly underbelly of life. Surely we can see that it was his sincere Christian perspective that made it possible for him to be thankful in spite of the evident anguish of the occasion.

Even the things that seem bad at the time can prove to be blessings in disguise. That is the reason that we ought to be continuously grateful. It should characterize our general attitude, not just be the thing that we say at the dinner table over our plentiful supply of "good eats."

In southern Alabama is the town of Enterprise, in Coffee County. There they have erected a monument to an insect, the Mexican boll weevil. In 1895 cotton was the major crop of the county, and the boll weevil began a systematic infestation that threatened to destroy the wealth of the region. In desperation to survive, the farmers were forced to diversify their crops, and by the year 1919 the county's peanut crop was many times what the cotton crop had been at its height. In that year of prosperity, a fountain and monument were built. It reads: "In profound appreciation of the boll weevil and what it has done as the herald of prosperity this monument was erected by the citizens of Enterprise, Coffee County, Alabama." Out of struggle and crisis had come new growth and success. Out of adversity had come blessing.

The Psalmist exhorted the worshipers of his era to "be thankful unto him, and bless his (God's) name" (Ps. 100:4). Paul condemned the pagans because of their egregious moral failures, but also because they were not thankful to God for the good things they had to enjoy (Rom. 1:21). That same writer went on to point out that Christian people are called into one spiritual body and it is expected of them that at the very least they will be thankful to God for their blessings (Col. 3:15). In fact, they ought to "abound in thanksgiving" (Col. 2:7). Communication with God should include, "prayer and supplication with thanksgiving" (Phil. 4:6). Apparently it is easy for us to ask for what we want, but far more difficult to be mindful and therefore grateful for what we have already received!

The story is told of a man and his wife who gave a sizeable contribution to a certain church to honor the memory of their son who had lost his life in the war. When the announcement was made of this very generous donation, a woman in the audience had a flash of inspiration and with her eyes open wide, whispered to her husband, "Let's give the same amount for our boy!" Her husband looked at her in total confusion, "What are you talking about? Our son was not killed." She answered back warmly, "That is just the point! Let's give it as an expression of our gratitude to God for sparing his life!" How often are we like this? It never crosses our minds to honor God for the good things that we take for granted, that are given to us in such abundance, that fill our lives day by day. Others who are not so blessed will readily tell us how extremely fortunate we are, while we fail to recognize on our own how truly privileged we are.

On the tombstone of her husband's grave, a Southern mountain woman had chiseled in rough and uneven letters this epitaph: "He always appreciated." The fact that this man was grateful for all of the favors done for him by his beloved wife, touched this woman's heart and was the most memorable thing about their relationship. So much so, that she had it inscribed on his gravestone for all to read. On the other hand, Leslie Flynn tells the story of a Vermont farmer, who was sitting on the porch of their farmhouse with his wife. He was beginning to realize how much she meant to him. It was about time, for they had already lived together for over forty-two years, and she had been a marvelous helper. She had proven herself a faithful companion to him, and a very willing and capable worker on the farm throughout their life together. Deep in reflection, he haltingly said to her, "Wife, you have been such a wonderful woman that there are times that I can hardly keep from telling you!" Sad to say, more often than not we are like this Vermont farmer and little like the Southern mountain man. Certainly much more often than we would like to admit. For whatever reason, we fail to tell God how much he means to us. And even when we do, our clumsy words fall short of saying what really deserves to be said. We neglect sincerely and clearly to tell him, "Thank you."

William Law, in his book *A Serious Call to a Devout and Holy Life* asked the question, "Who is the greatest saint in the world?" In answer to this he said, "It is he who is always thankful to God, who wills everything that God willeth, who receives everything as an instance of God's goodness, and has a heart always ready to praise God for it."

But, as we mentioned earlier, there is another side to all of this also. This has more to do with the person who is thankful than the One to Whom he or she is thankful. Thankfulness and happiness go hand in hand. The two walk together down many a lonely mile of life's way. Happiness, as much as anything else in the world, is associated with

NOTES:

the feeling and concrete expression of gratitude. Do not miss this important secret to contentment. We cannot proffer an expression of gratitude and in the same breath complain about our situation. These two things have no relationship to one another. They are in fact polar opposites. So, practice the habit of being grateful, of counting your blessings, and you will be headed merrily down the road that leads to happiness.

Questions

1. Do you agree with the author's opinion that modern society has "coarsened" in recent years? Can you provide some illustrations to prove your view? Or, will they make you blush? _____
   _____

2. Has gratitude been one of the fine virtues that in your view has diminished or even disappeared in society? Can you offer some examples from your own experience? _____
   _____

3. Is it true that there is not any condition in the world so miserable but that one could find something for which to be grateful? Illustrate your answer. _____
   _____

4. Discuss the importance of thankfulness from God's perspective. As the One who "gives to all liberally" (Jas. 1:6), how might God see things differently than we who are the beneficiaries of so many good things from his hands? _____
   _____

5. What passages of Scripture impress us with the importance of thankfulness, besides the ones cited by the author? _____
   _____

6. Do thankfulness and happiness really go hand in hand? How would you illustrate this point? Would a person who is ungrateful tend also to be unhappy? Why or why not? _____
   _____
   _____

7. Spend a few moments "counting your blessings." Write them down. After you have done so, does this tend, almost immediately, to make you more conscious of God's good gifts to you? _____
   _____
   _____
   _____

Act Like You Are Happy

Sometimes it is hard to tell whether people are happy or not. The most visible sign of happiness is a smile. It is difficult to argue or quarrel with laughter. One smile tends to beget another in someone else. All of us take pleasure in the company of happy people. None of us enjoys the company of those who are depressed and despondent, especially when they are continually so. We may spend time with them to help them out of their depression, but we will also tend to work hard to avoid their presence if we can.

"Sometimes your joy is the source of your smile, but sometimes your smile can be the source of your joy," wrote Thich Nhat Hanh. If we are happy, we ought to act like we are. One fellow asked his sad-looking friend, "Do you feel alright?" "Why, yes," came the reply. "Well, if you feel fine, why don't you notify your face?"

Acting like we are happy will actually change our mood from sadness to joy. If a person changes his facial expression to a smile, the mind will tend to follow suit. This is a simple act of will, which can alter the entire mental outlook of almost anyone. Dr. George W. Crane, speaking of marital attitudes in his book *Applied Psychology*, had this to say on the matter of physical actions leading to changes in the emotions of people: "Remember, motions are the precursors of emotions. You can't control the latter directly but only through

When we feel unhappy, if we will but smile and act happy, the result will be a complete change of mood and temperament.

your choice of motions or actions. . . .To avoid this all too common tragedy (marital difficulties and misunderstandings) become aware of the true psychological facts. Go through the proper motions each day and you'll soon begin to feel the corresponding emotions! Just be sure you and your mate go through those motions of dates and kisses, the phrasing of sincere daily compliments, plus the many other little courtesies, and you need not worry about the emotion of love. You can't act devoted for very long without feeling devoted."

Action, in a sense, is like a chemical catalyst within the brain. A catalyst is a substance that initiates a chemical reaction but is not itself consumed in the overall reaction. For example, many years ago a certain German laboratory was working toward a chemical method of producing indigo synthetically. Phthalic acid was needed as an intermediate chemical. It was reasoned that it ought to be possible to obtain it by treating naphthalene with fuming sulphuric acid. The theory seemed to be solid, and there was every expectation of success, but the result was consistently unfavorable. Neither heat nor pressure, nor anything else seemed to produce the desired effect. In the midst of one of the experiments, a young fellow employed in the laboratory as an assistant was told to take a reading from a thermometer. The boy clumsily dropped the thermometer and broke it, so that a few drops of mercury fell into the brew. Immediately, the liquid began to seethe and labor, and in a short while there was no naphthalene left; the container was full of the desired phthalic acid. Mercury was the catalyst that produced the desired chemical reaction!

Acting in a certain way is much like this. It is a catalyst that often results in the desired effect of changing the mood and emotion. Feelings tend to follow actions. In other words, we can change our attitudes by changing our physical actions. This is true in many different ways. For example, human beings feel more superior when they stand tall than when they slouch. When people are well dressed, they tend to exude confidence. On the negative side, if they are dressed in a slovenly manner they tend to behave with less self-assurance. In fact, if they simply contort their face into a really bitter frown, they will feel more like frowning. Here, then is the lesson: When we feel unhappy, if we will but smile and act happy, the result will be a complete change of mood and temperament. This is a simple but profound fact which can utterly change your life. If you will put it to the test, you will shortly begin to see how true it is and how remarkable are the dividends that it pays.

Have you ever been forced into a social situation where you have to be happy and talkative soon after an argument or an unpleasant confrontation with someone? Most of us have. Generally, we put on a smile and act as if nothing is the matter. We talk and laugh and put the matter entirely out of our mind for a time, and interestingly enough, soon the whole thing is entirely out of our mind. We are acting jovial and conversational, on account of the social requirements of the occasion, and that is precisely what we have become. When we have time all to ourselves once more, and have the opportunity to think about the unpleasantness again, it is not long until we are brooding and gloomy, we are downcast and melancholy, and depression is just around the corner. So, we have gone from sadness to joy and back to sadness again. The thing that took us from sadness to joy is a human situation which required that we *act like we are happy!* There is not one of us who can say that we have not played out this scenario on more than one occasion. In doing so, we have demonstrated that acting like we are happy is capable of transforming our mental state. It is therefore a simple matter of putting it to the test whenever we are downhearted and blue. "Just put on a happy face," says a popular song, and it may actually be just that simple sometimes!

Moreover, it can actually have physical repercussions as well. Good health may be one of the most important benefits. The Bible says, "A cheerful heart is a good medicine; but a broken spirit dries up the bones" (Prov. 17:22). Medical professionals have often observed that the mental outlook of a patient can make a tremendous difference in the outcome of almost any procedure. University of Toronto researchers, who recently published their results in *Psycho-Ontology*, interviewed 300 women who had been cancer-free for at least two years. They asked the women what they think caused the disease and what they've done to prevent its return. More than 40% of the women blamed stress for the disease's onset over scientifically linked factors such as genetics and environment. The study also showed 60% believe a positive attitude has kept them healthy. "We were surprised," says lead researcher Donna Stewart, M.D., the women's health chair at the University Health Network. "We had no idea positive attitude was going to be as high as it turned out to be."

Of course, this is not a guarantee of positive results, but it certainly increases the chances of positive results. In addition, the general experience of medical treatment, as frightening and painful as it may sometimes be, takes on a completely different aspect when it is attended by an attitude that sees the process in the best and most favorable light.

If you want to be happy, then *act like it!*

Questions

1. Is it true that "acting like you are happy can actually change your mood from sadness to joy"? Is this just a theory from "pop psychology," or is this merely a simple and easily provable observation from human experience? Frankly, the best way to establish which one is correct, is to try it out. Have you tried it? _____

   _____

2. The wise man said, "A cheerful heart is a good medicine; but a broken spirit dries up the bones" (Prov. 17:22). Have you known of cases personally where this principle was at work? Have you seen it in your own life? _____

   _____

3. Have you ever been put in a social situation where you had to act happy in spite of your true inner mood? Did your somber mood change, at least for the time being? What is the lesson we may learn from this? Are we willing to make a few necessary changes to our outward circumstances in order to enjoy a better inward attitude and, therefore, a generally better morale? _____

   _____

4. Years ago, I knew a man in the church whose wife passed away. He was a fellow in his mid fifties and in generally good health. The two had been a wonderfully happy Christian couple who loved the Lord and were very faithful to the church. After her death, he confided to me that he no longer had anything to live for. He said that he wished the Lord would take him soon. Within two years he was dead from cancer. Did he die from loneliness, grief, and sadness, or did God hear his prayer and give him the desire of his heart (read Psa. 10:17; 38:9; 145:19; Prov. 10:24)? Could it have been a combination of the two? Be careful what you ask for! _____

   _____

5. My own great aunt was in the hospital when she learned the news that her husband had been killed in an unfortunate traffic accident. She told her daughter, "Now that Daddy is gone, I can go too. I have just tried to stay alive long enough to take care of him." She never left the hospital. She died in that room two days later. Do you know of any cases like this? What does this say about our own good health, or lack thereof, and does it also say something generally true about human longevity?

   _____

   _____

   _____

Concentrate on Solutions Rather Than Problems

Every life has a certain number of problems. Perhaps it could even be said that every day of every week has a certain number of problems associated with it. Taking this view of things, life is really all about problem solving. Many years ago people awoke every morning with the problem of where to get the next meal. Day laborers rose with the sun to face the problem of getting work for that single day so they could provide food for themselves and their families. The main problem of life was daily survival. As hard as it may be for you to imagine, there are places in this world where people faced that same reality this very morning.

In the face of that circumstance, Jesus warned his disciples, "Be not anxious for your life, what you shall eat, or what you shall drink; nor yet for your body, what you shall put on. Is not the life more than the food, and the body than the raiment? Behold, the birds of the heaven, that they sow not, neither do they reap, nor gather into barns; and your heavenly Father feeds them. Are not you of much more value than they?" (Matt. 6:25, 26).

On some of the Caribbean islands, the phrase, "Don't worry, be happy" is frequently quoted. This little line of folk wisdom has much to teach us. Too often we are burdened with or even consumed by a perpetual preoccupation with all of the terrible things which *might* happen. Most of them never will. In the words of an old farmer, "Most of the stuff people worry about ain't never gonna happen, anyway." The ones that do, we will deal with one at a time as they come our way.

The word *worry* is from an Anglo-Saxon term meaning "to choke or strangle." Moreover, that is precisely what worry does. It chokes the happiness out of living our lives. Our worry will not help us at all. It will only steal away the joys and pleasures of today. Paul said, "In nothing be anxious; but in everything by prayer

> "Most of the stuff people worry about ain't never gonna happen, anyway."

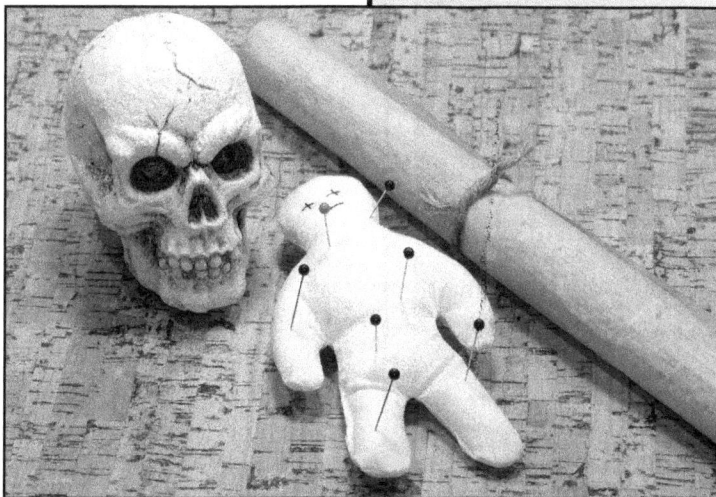

_____
_____
_____
_____
_____
_____
_____
_____
_____
_____
_____
_____
_____
_____
_____
_____
_____
_____
_____
_____

> **Jesus wanted his disciples to spend their energies upon the solutions, rather than centering their thoughts upon the negatives.**

and supplication with thanksgiving, let your requests be made known to God. And the peace of God, which passes all understanding, shall guard your hearts and your thoughts in Christ Jesus" (Phil. 4:6-7). The Psalmist rejoiced in his victory over doubt and fear, and explained its disappearance from his life thus: "I sought the Lord and he heard me, and delivered me from all my fears" (Ps. 34:4). In another place, he said that God was "a very present help in trouble" (Ps. 46:1). God is the ultimate solution to our many problems, especially our fretting and worrying, but we will often suffer for a long time in silence, never making our appeal for relief before the heavenly court. The marvelous truth is that God *wants* us to ask him for help! He himself said, "Call upon me in the day of trouble; I will deliver you, and you shall glorify me" (Ps. 50:15); again, "The Lord is near all those who call upon him, to all who call upon him in truth; he will fulfill the desire of those who fear him. He also will hear their cry and save them; the Lord preserves all those who love him" (Ps. 145:18-20). These are divine promises that will sustain us in the most difficult of times. In order for them to sustain us, though, we must claim them; and for us to claim them we must know and believe them through and through. One or more of these passages of Sacred Scripture ought to be committed to memory and repeated to ourselves over and over whenever our hearts are filled with doubt or anxiety.

The power that fretfulness can have over us should not be underestimated. Dr. Norman Vincent Peale offered an illustration of how negative energy in the form of worry can actually destroy a life. He wrote:

> When worry becomes really acute, it can clamp down on the mind like a vise, blotting out all rational thought processes. This is how black magic works. A friend of mine who lives in South Africa once told me how his mother's maid became convinced that a local witch doctor had put a spell on her because she had offended him in some manner. She became unable to eat because all food seemed to have a terrible odor, although actually it didn't. Everything edible became repulsive to her. She was convinced that she was going to die, and although her employers called in doctors and ministers to help her, she finally did die of starvation—so powerful were the negative images that had taken possession of her mind (*How to Make Positive Imaging Work for You*, 60).

This same terrible result has frequently been observed in various cultures. It has come to be called "Voodoo Death." Soares de Sousa in South America was the first to observe instances of this sort of death among the Tupinambás Indians, evidently induced by fright when men were condemned and sentenced by a so-called "medicine man." In Brown's *New Zealand and Its Aborigines* there is an account of a Maori woman who, having eaten some fruit, was told that it had been taken from a tabooed place; she exclaimed that the sanctity of the chief had been profaned and that his spirit would kill her. This incident occurred in the afternoon; the next day about 12 o'clock she was dead. According to Tregear the *tapu* (taboo) among the Maoris of New Zealand is an awful weapon. "I have seen a strong young man die," he declared, "the same day he was tapued; the victims die under it as though their strength ran out as water."

Dr. S. M. Lambert of the Western Pacific Health Service of the Rockefeller Foundation wrote that on several occasions he had seen evidence of death from fear. In one case there was a startling recovery. At a Mission at Mona Mona in North Queensland were many native converts, but on the outskirts of the Mission was a group of non-converts including one Nebo, a famous witch doctor. The chief helper of the missionary was Rob, a native who had been converted. When Dr. Lambert arrived at the Mission he learned that Rob was in distress and that the missionary wanted him examined. Dr. Lambert made the examination, and found no fever, no complaint of pain, no symptoms, and no signs of disease. He was impressed, however, by the obvious indications that Rob was seriously ill and extremely weak. From the missionary he learned that Rob had had a bone pointed at him by Nebo and was convinced that in consequence he must die. Thereupon Dr. Lambert and the missionary went for Nebo, threatened him sharply that his supply of food would be shut off if anything happened to Rob and that he and his people would be driven away from the Mission. At once Nebo agreed to go with them to see Rob. He leaned over Rob's bed and told the sick man that it was all a mistake, a mere joke—indeed, that he had not pointed a bone at him at all. The relief, Dr. Lambert testified, was almost instantaneous; that evening Rob was back at work, quite happy again, and in full possession of his physical strength (From "Voodoo death," *American Antropologist* [1942]: 44 [new series]:169-181). All of this illustrates in the most unambiguous way possible the power that is inherent in the formidable emotions of fear and worry. Both of them have the power to kill and destroy us from within.

Unfortunately, there is a very strong tendency in the human mind to concentrate upon the problems that confront us in life. Jesus wanted his disciples to spend their energies upon the solutions, rather than centering their thoughts upon the negatives. We are to do what we must to earn a living, but after that it is important that we not frustrate our minds by an oppressive concentration upon the problems of life. David said, "I have been young, and now am old; yet I have not seen the righteous forsaken, nor his seed begging bread" (Ps. 37:25). God provides solutions to our problems.

On one occasion Elisha, the prophet's servant, arose to find that they were surrounded on all sides by the Syrian hosts. They were trapped. The situation seemed absolutely hopeless. When he was told of it, Elisha responded, "Fear not; for they that are with us are more than they that are with them." The prophet then prayed that the young man's eyes might be opened, and when God opened his eyes, the Bible says, "And he saw, and behold, the mountain was full of horses and chariots of fire round about Elisha" (2 Kings 6:14-17). The servant was seeing only the problem. Elisha was fixated upon the solution. God was taking care of them and seeing to their needs. He had already made provision for their deliverance, and Elisha knew this and was not concerned in the least. Too many of us are like the servant who was blind to God's power and care; and far too few of us are like Elisha who trusted God even when things seemed hopeless. It is incredibly important that we not overspend our energies on the problems we encounter, especially to the neglect of the solutions that may be readily apparent when we open our eyes to see them.

1. In Matthew 6:25, 26 Jesus warned his disciples not to worry over the necessities of life: food, clothing, or shelter. These are the most fundamental needs of life. In ancient societies people labored for a single day's wages, and concerned themselves primarily with whether they would have enough to eat today and then the same again tomorrow. In some third-world societies they do the same in our time. Do we live under this cloud of fear in our own society today? Does this make it difficult for us to sympathize with such folk in modern times? _____

_____

2. Is your own life full of problems? What are some of them? Could it be accurately said that life is really about problem solving? If it is, should we not try to get better at it? _____

_____

3. Is it true that most of the bad things people imagine happening never really do? Can you think of something terrible that you thought was going to happen, but it never actually came to pass? _____

_____

4. Discuss the implications for our lives of the following texts of Scripture: Phil. 4:6-7; Pss. 34:4; 46:1; 50:15; 145:18-20. Does God want us to ask him for help in our personal times of struggle? Is it wrong for us to fret and agonize over personal problems when he has promised us help for just such times as this? Which one of these passages will you commit to memory in order to repeat it over and over when you begin to obsess over some problem in your life? _____

_____

_____

5. Where does the power of "black magic" or "voodoo" lie? Is it in the power of the so-called magic itself, or in the power of the mind to be frightened by it? _____

_____

6. Do you know someone who has been sickened, weakened, even paralyzed by the powerful emotions of fear and worry? To what degree do these emotions control your own life? Is this indicative of weak faith? _____

_____

7. What are some of the powerful promises of God that address these destructive emotions in our lives? If these promises are available and we do not call upon them, would it be any different if they were not there at all? How do you think God views all of this? _____

_____

8. Read together the story related in 2 Kings 6:8-23 of the Syrian raiding parties who thought they had Elisha the prophet in a death grip, only to find that God had provided rescue for the prophet and capture for them. What are the important lessons that we ought to learn about God's providence and loving care for his people? How important is it that we "open our eyes" in order to see these spiritual realities? _____

_____

"As From the Outside Looking In"

One of our most formidable problems as far as happiness is concerned is our own inability to see ourselves as others do, or even as God does. In whatever circumstance we find ourselves, we lack the necessary "peripheral vision" to view it as perhaps even we would if someone else were undergoing the experience. If someone else has toenail surgery, the whole thing seems rather unimportant. We may even ask ourselves, "Why is she making such a big deal of this?" But if it is *me* having toenail surgery, then it takes on an entirely different perspective. In any situation where I am directly involved, a relatively insignificant matter takes on monumental significance. Molehills tend to become mountains when they are *my* molehills.

Astronaut Russell Schweikart noted regarding his view of earth from outer space: "You see the Earth as a bright blue and white Christmas tree ornament in the black sky. It's so small and so fragile—you realize that on that small spot is everything that means everything to you; all of history and art and death and birth and love." Most of us will never see this planet from the dark nether regions of outer space, but almost all of us have flown. Have you ever taken a plane flight far above the earth on a clear and cloudless day, and wondered at how small everything seems to be so far down below? Have you imagined what people might be doing as they make their way in the world down there, each in his own tiny little corner of the planet? Here is a person who is scratching and clawing to get to the top of a corporate ladder, to receive top pay, and get all of the recognition that goes along with it. There is someone who is working all day and late into the evening, sacrificing his home life and the intimacy of his beloved family in order to get to the top of his profession. Over there is someone, at all costs, whether by hook or crook, desperately striving to win a sales contest, to get a plaque for his wall, and a trip to some exciting and exotic destination. In still another little corner, barely visible from so high up, there is a young man or young woman who wants so much to impress a certain person of the opposite sex that they dream about them all night long and fantasize about them during the day. How extremely insignificant

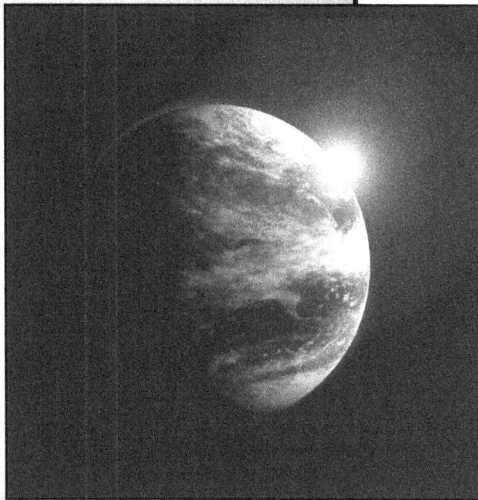

it all seems from up so high! From our own little cubicle at the office it all seems so very important, but from an outsider's viewpoint it takes on a completely different aspect.

When we are flying above it all, we have a "bird's-eye view" of the world. From that vantage point everything looks different. It seems so small and unimpressive from up so high. Surely this must be how God sees many of the troubles and problems in our experience. This is not to say that God does not care about us, for he has certainly said in many different ways that he cares profoundly about our lives, and wants us to share those burdens with him: "Cast all of your anxiety upon him, for he cares for you" (1 Pet. 5:7). However, for us to deal with the difficulties we experience in life it is important that we have an accurate estimation of their true proportions, or lack thereof. Many of the things we worry over, lose sleep about, and generally wreck our health on account of, if looked at from a different angle would seem to be too insignificant for all of the fuss we make over them. If we could only be persuaded to take a look at these things "from above," as it were, we would sometimes laugh at ourselves for some of the cases of our own lack of realistic perspective in viewing these things in their true light.

In the biblical book of Job, the great patriarch with whom the book is primarily concerned suffers the most horrible experiences that life could throw at him. He loses all of his possessions, his children are all killed tragically, and his health is lost at about the same time. His wife has become bitter and hostile toward his religious faith, considering it nothing more than a futile exercise. He sits in utter desperation and misery throughout most of the book. As a result of his dreadful sufferings, and the hateful accusations of his friends who supposedly came to "comfort" him, this righteous man began to wallow in self pity and even to accuse God of being unfair in his own particular case.

In the end God broke his long silence and spoke to Job "out of a whirlwind." In doing so, he did not explain his own actions to Job, for God does not owe an explanation of his ways to any human being. However, he asked Job many questions about the universe and its wonders, questions that no human being could ever answer. In essence, if only momentarily, he took Job outside of himself, and outside his unique personal perspective. Looking at the matter from God's side of the table, he recognized that he had spoken of things that he did not understand, "things too wonderful for me, which I knew not" (Job 42:3). In the end, he repented of his proud accusations, and was restored to God's favor (Job 42:6ff.). The key to his change of viewpoint was his willingness to step outside of his own wretchedness long enough to consider the matter objectively.

> NOTES:

> **The key to his change of viewpoint was his willingness to step outside of his own wretchedness long enough to consider the matter objectively.**

If we could only learn something from the book of Job, and view our own lives as others see them, or even better, as God might see them, then happiness might more easily be attained. In other words, looking at things "as from the outside looking in," will give us a superior perspective on our lives and our actions.

Therefore, do your best to stay detached, especially when things do not proceed as intended or desired. Detachment will help you to stay calm and control your moods and reactions. Understand something important about this thing called "detachment," however; it is not exactly the same as indifference. Rather, it is the acceptance of the good as well as the bad while staying balanced whichever way things go. Detachment has much to do with the attainment of inner peace, and inner peace most assuredly is conducive to the enjoyment of happiness.

Questions

1. Discuss the relative significance or lack thereof pertaining to our own personal problems and difficulties, our triumphs and tragedies, our hopes and dreams. Are we able to distinguish the difference between which of these is important and which ones are not? How differently might God see them? Do we see things in the same way and from the same perspective as God does? Which ones? Why this difference? _____

   _____

2. Does God care about all of the problems of all of the people in the world? Does God concern himself with the toothache of an Australian in Sidney? Does he consider important the fact that a child has polio in Ghana? Does he grieve that a man has lost his wife and is left alone and childless in the Republic of Equador? Does he sympathize with a girl in Chicago who has been embarrassed and wounded by the painful remarks of a supposed friend? How does each of these things bear upon our understanding of 1 Peter 5:7? _____

   _____

3. Discuss the various tragedies of Job's life (Job 1:6-19; 2:1-10, 11-3:1-5) in the light of God's concern for Job's trouble and sorrow. Why did God ask the ancient patriarch the long list of questions that he did in Job 38:1-40:2? What was he trying to get Job to realize? _____

4. What is the importance of Job's humble remarks spoken in the middle of God's speeches in 40:3-5? Why was God not satisfied with them? Why did God go on to offer one more extended speech and two more powerful examples of Job's weakness in the face of God's mighty creation (behemoth and leviathan in 40:6-41:34)? _____

   _____

5. Was God satisfied with Job's second, more self-deprecating statement in Job 42:1-6? How do you know? What do you think the explanation of this is?_____

   _____

6. Is it easy to remain "detached" from the events of your own life? Why is it important to attempt to do so? _____

   _____

Define Life's Purpose

For many people who live today life seems wholly futile and absolutely senseless. "What is the use of living? What's it all about anyway?" they ask. This feeling is not something new or unique to the modern era. Every age has faced it apart from a confident knowledge of God the Creator. In his moments of seeming abandonment, Job professed, "Let the day perish wherein I was born, and the night which said, 'There is a man-child conceived'" (Job 3:3). In his deep despair, the author of Ecclesiastes wrote, "Vanity of vanities, says the Preacher; all is vanity" (12:8). Carlyle opined, "A man without a purpose is like a ship without a rudder—a waif, a nothing, a no man." These words are true and quite beyond any controversy. There is nothing new about this feeling of emptiness and aimlessness. It is as old as the human experience.

A hammer fits the hand of a man; clearly it is made for hammering nails into wood. Pull another tool from the toolbox, and another after that. Each one has its own clearly definable purpose. It is shaped and fitted to some particular usage. The hand of man is for grasping and holding. The eye is for seeing. The ear is for hearing. The nose is for smelling. The mouth is for talking and eating. What is *my* purpose? What is the whole of me for? What *is* life? What *is* it about? Why *are* we here? What *ought we to do* with the time we have between birth and death? These are valid and perfectly legitimate questions which have haunted men throughout the generations. The fact that we are intellectually capable of posing such questions and attempting to answer them suggests two things. First, it suggests that we are somehow superior to the lower creation, ordinary animals like dogs and cats, as sophisticated and "smart" as they may sometimes seem. Dogs and cats do not puzzle over such matters. Given a few quiet moments to contemplate their existence, either one will fall fast asleep before the process of thinking has begun.

Human beings are clearly different. We think a great deal about such things. We reason back and forth, we even argue relentlessly about them. Animals might fight over a scrap of meat, but it is inconceivable for them to quarrel over why they exist and whether there is some purpose for their being. Christ stated the necessary logical consequence of this: "Are not you of much more value than they?" (Matt.

> "A man without a purpose is like a ship without a rudder—a waif, a nothing, a no man."
>
> — *Carlyle*

> "The majority of men live without being thoroughly conscious that they are spiritual beings."
>
> — *Soren Kierkegaard*

_____

_____

_____

_____

_____

_____

_____

_____

_____

_____

_____

_____

_____

_____

_____

_____

_____

_____

_____

_____

_____

_____

> **Human beings have a deep-seated need to understand that they are here for some useful purpose.**

6:26). Human beings are not only a higher order of being, but they also have a higher order of worth. Most of us would prefer to see a hundred alligators destroyed than to see a single human child consumed by a hungry reptile. It is a simple matter of worth. Most of us find the outrageous comparisons made by PETA advocates abhorrent in the extreme. A small minority may be swayed by their rhetoric, but most of us remain unconvinced. We see plainly and manifestly the difference between an animal and a human being, and we value the human far above the animal.

Second, it suggests that we are here for more than just eating, drinking, and procreating. "Great minds have purposes, little minds have wishes," observed Washington Irving. Since we are a higher being, possessed of the ability to contemplate our existence, there must surely be a reason for us to be here that is higher and nobler than that of the lower animals. Human beings cannot be satisfied with eating, drinking, and procreating—oh, certainly there are some people who can get along fine without much thought for the reason of things. But most of us cannot be happy with minimal expectations. We want something more for ourselves than a scrap of meat to fight over. Jesus said, "Is not the life more than the food, and the body than the raiment?" (Matt. 6:25). The answer to his simple but profound question is, "Yes!" There is far more to life than just the food we eat. Life is more than merely a physical phenomenon that can be explained entirely in terms of its biological processes. People who are thoughtful know intuitively that life must be related to something beyond itself for it to be meaningful. Yet, as the Danish theologian Soren Kierkegaard suggested, "The majority of men live without being thoroughly conscious that they are spiritual beings."

Ivan Ilich is the main character in the Leo Tolstoy story *The Death of Ivan Ilich,* often considered the greatest novella in Russian literature. Literary works in Tolstoy's time were usually judged by how well they promoted some ideological agenda, and Ivan Ilich was frequently read as a critique of the banal materialism and insincerity that dominated privileged bourgeois culture. In fact, it is the story of a worldly careerist, a high court judge who had never given the inevitability of his death so much as a passing thought. But one day death announced itself to him, and to his shocked surprise he was brought face to face with his own mortality. How, Tolstoy asks, does an unreflective man confront his one and only moment of truth? The perfect bureaucrat, Ivan Ilich treasured his orderly domestic and official routine. Diagnosed with an incurable illness, he at first denied the truth, but influenced by the simple acceptance of his servant Gerasim, Ivan Ilich eventually came to embrace the boy's belief that death is natural and not somehow shameful. He comforted himself with happy memories of childhood and gradually realized that he had ignored all his inner yearnings as he tried to do what was expected of him. Ivan was a very normal person who always did everything that was ever expected of him, but he was never happy. He hated his life; he hated his wife; he hated everything about his pitiful existence. Unfortunately, he never realized this until it was too late to change any of it. Social pressures and material success blinded him to reality. Therefore, he died wondering, "What if my whole life was wrong?" Gary L. Jahn insightfully commented regarding the message of this important work of Tolstoy (A Critical Companion): "Faith still remained for me as irrational as it was before, but I could not but admit that it alone gives people a reply to the questions of life, and that consequently it makes life possible." He went on to explain that this conviction makes possible a saving belief in God: "To know God and to live are one and the same. God is life." Many people are exactly like Ivan Ilich in their approach to existence; they never take the time to reflect upon what it all may mean and whether there may be some purpose to life. Also like Ivan, they wait until it is too late for them to make a difference by making some adjustments in the direction of their life.

Scripture tells us that man enjoys a unique relationship with God, unlike the lower creation, and that in consequence of that relationship he bears responsibility for how his life is conducted. The wise man in Ecclesiastes explained it thus: "This is the end of the matter; all has been heard: Fear God, and keep his commandments; for this is the whole duty of man. For God will bring every work into judgment, with every hidden thing, whether it be good or evil" (12:13, 14). There is no word for "duty" in the original Hebrew text of this verse. It therefore means, "this is the whole of man." This is it. It is the *summum bonum*, the chief good. We need look no further for a higher purpose; this is our purpose.

Benjamin Franklin (1706-1790) was one of the leading founding fathers of the United States of America. He signed both the *Declaration of Independence* and the *Constitution*, and served as the new nation's ablest diplomat. Franklin's formal schooling ended early but his education never did. He believed that "the doors to wisdom are never shut," and read every book he could get his hands on. Franklin taught himself simple algebra and geometry, navigation, logic, history, science, English grammar, and a working knowledge of five other languages. Franklin had a simple formula for success. He believed that successful people worked just a little harder than other people. Benjamin Franklin certainly did. He built a successful printing and publishing business in Philadelphia; he conducted scientific studies of electricity and made several important discoveries; he was an accomplished diplomat and statesman; he helped establish Pennsylvania's first university and America's first city hospital. He also organized the country's

NOTES:

> "Faith still remained for me as irrational as it was before, but I could not but admit that it alone gives people a reply to the questions of life, and that consequently it makes life possible."
>
> — *Tolstoy*

first subscription library. Franklin was also unequaled in America as an inventor until Thomas Edison. He invented the Franklin stove, bifocal eyeglasses, and the lightning rod. Franklin was not greedy about his inventions, preferring to have them used freely for the comfort and convenience of everyone. He also had a strong belief that good citizenship included an obligation of public service. Franklin himself served the city of Philadelphia, Pennsylvania and the new United States of America, in one way or the other, for most of his life. To Benjamin Franklin there was no greater purpose in life than to "live usefully."

Thomas Alva Edison was born on February 11, 1847 in Milan, Ohio. With only three months of formal education he became one of the greatest inventors and industrial leaders in history. Edison obtained 1,093 United States patents, the most issued to any individual. Edison's greatest contribution was the first practical electric lighting. He not only invented the first successful electric light bulb, but also set up the first electrical power distribution company. Edison invented the phonograph, and made improvements to the telegraph, telephone, and motion picture technology. He also founded the first modern research laboratory. Over time he also proved to be a very capable businessman and a fierce competitor in marketing his inventions.

These two men, Benjamin Franklin and Thomas Edison, illustrate the importance of purpose in the life of man. Admittedly both of these men were extraordinary individuals, endowed with special talents and astonishing intellects. Few people in the history of the human family will compare very favorably with their genius or work ethic. At the same time, they both have one thing in common. They were possessed with a clear vision of where they wanted to go, where they were headed, even if they did not always know at first how to get there. Carl Sandburg said, "Nothing happens unless first we dream." Ella Wheeler Wilcox wrote:

> One ship sails East,
> And another West,
> By the self-same winds that blow,
> Tis the set of the sails
> And not the gales,
> That tells the way we go.

Human beings have a deep-seated need to understand that they are here for some useful purpose. When they are able to discern that purpose, then they may prove to be enormously fruitful and prolific in steering themselves toward some worthy goal. Lacking some appreciation for his purpose, some comprehension of his *raison d'etre*, some hint that he is not an empty ship headed nowhere on a sea of nothingness, he can wind up an intellectual and emotional derelict. In our time many are doing just that.

Man has a reason for being here, and it has been defined in terms of something more than mere survival. Eating, drinking, and procreating are relegated to the background when one's real reason for existing is considered. Jesus said, "I am the bread of life; he who comes to me shall never hunger, and he who believes in me shall never thirst" (John 6:35). Something in God answers to the deep needs of man and fills his life with meaning and purpose. God created man and did not leave him to his own resources to determine why he is here and what he ought to be about while he is around. God has informed him as to what he must do with his time on earth. He has important business for him to conduct during his stay. Too, he will give an account of his stewardship of his time at some unannounced future date.

In the parables of Jesus the Lord frequently described the relationship between God and man as that of a wealthy nobleman or landowner who left for a far country. In each case he departs, leaving his servant in charge of certain obligations; upon returning he asked that the servant give an account of his stewardship (cf. Luke 19:12ff.; etc.). This is most clearly a caricature of how God sees us in our relationship to himself.

Paul saw it in terms of a goal towards which we need to be striving. He expressed it this way: "I press on toward the goal unto the prize of the high calling of God in Christ Jesus" (Phil. 3:14). We are not here for a good time only; we have promises to keep. Happiness will always seem out of reach if we have not been able correctly to define life's purpose.

> Something in God answers to the deep needs of man and fills his life with meaning and purpose.

Questions

1. What are the implications of Job's exclamation, "Let the day perish wherein I was born, and the night which said, 'There is a man-child conceived'" (Job 3:3)? _____

   _____

2. What was the background and setting for the following statement in Ecclesiastes 12:8, "Vanity of vanities, says the preacher; all is vanity"? _____

   _____

3. Every part of the human anatomy has a purpose. What is the purpose of the whole? In other words, what is your purpose for being here in this world? Is it illogical to argue that the whole of man has no reason for its existence? _____

   _____

4. If man does have a purpose for existing, then how do we go about discovering that purpose? Is it reasonable to expect that our Creator has somewhere, somehow, revealed that purpose to us? Would it be just or reasonable for him to expect anything at all from us and yet never tell us of his expectation? _____

   _____

5. What are some of the differences between lower animals and human beings? _____

   _____

6. Do these differences fit well into the description of man and the lower creation that is found in the Bible? _____

7. Radical "animal rights" advocates claim there is no distinction to be made between the death of an animal and the death of a human child. How does this square with the Genesis account of the creation? How does it fit in with the theory of organic evolution? How does it square with the Lord's question in Matthew 6:26? _____

   _____

8. Does human life have value in an eternal sense, or is it merely existing that is important, i.e. breathing, eating, drinking and procreating? _____

   _____

9. Was Kierkegaard correct when he observed, "The majority of men live without being thoroughly conscious that they are spiritual beings"? Does it make a difference one way or the other? Explain your answer. _____

   _____

10. Is it true that most people are like Ivan Illich in Leo Tolstoy's novel, in that they in the hustle and bustle of life never pause to reflect upon what life is all about and whether there may actually be more to life than ordinary duty and responsibility? _____

   _____

11. Read Ecclesiastes 12:13, 14. Analyze this text in terms of the ultimate purpose of every individual. __

   _____

   _____

   _____

12. Look at the examples of Benjamin Franklin and Thomas Alva Edison in the light of a person appreciating their purpose in life. When one's purpose is clear and clearly defined, he can be enormously prolific. When he cannot seem to concentrate on one thing specifically and cannot seem to come to terms with the notion of purpose, then where will he wind up? Is defining your own purpose in life important to you? _____

   _____

13. Examine each of the following Scripture passages in the light of the question of purpose: John 6:35; Luke 19:12ff.; Phil. 3:14. _____

   _____

   _____

Locate and Focus Upon Life's Center

When Jesus was transfigured before the apostles Peter, James, and John, in the fervor of the moment Peter spoke of his desire to make three shrines in the place, "one for you (Jesus), and one for Moses, and one for Elijah" (Matt. 17:4). The fisherman apostle thought he was exalting Jesus by this exclamation, but in reality he was bringing him down to a human level. A voice from the cloud pronounced, "This is my beloved Son, in whom I am well pleased—hear him!" (v. 5).

In our own personal search for life's center, we need to keep this message in mind. Hearing him is more important than anything else. Paul said that "He is before all things, and in him all things consist. And he is the head of the body, the church: who is the beginning, the firstborn from the dead; that in all things he might have the preeminence" (Col. 1:17-18). If we put anything or anyone ahead of him in life, we are failing to keep him in his proper place, and so our lives will be out of sorts. He has not changed his position. He is still exactly where he has always been, for our lack of a proper view of him does not affect him at all. Our own view of things, however, is out of focus if we do not see him at the center.

It is reported that one evening the great conductor Arturo Toscanini conducted Beethoven's Ninth Symphony. It was a brilliant performance on the part of everyone involved. At the end, the audience was ecstatic. They clapped, whistled, and stomped their feet, caught up in the utter greatness of the performance. As Toscanini stood before the crowd, he bowed repeatedly, and then acknowledged his marvelous orchestra. When the ovation finally began to subside, the conductor turned and looked intently at his musicians. He was almost beside himself as he whispered to them, "Gentlemen! Gentlemen!" The orchestra leaned forward to listen. Was he angry? Was he proud? They could not tell. In a fiercely enunciated whisper, Toscanini said, "Gentlemen, I am nothing!" This was an extraordinary admission since he was blessed with amazing musical genius and an enormous ego. He added, "Gentlemen, you are nothing." They had heard this same message many times before during rehearsal. "But Beethoven," said Toscanini, in a tone of absolute adoration, "is

> "The supreme happiness of life is the conviction that we are loved—loved for ourselves, or rather, loved in spite of ourselves."
>
> — *Victor Hugo*

> If we put anything or anyone ahead of him in life, we are failing to keep him in his proper place, and so our lives will be out of sorts.

everything, everything, everything!" Toscanini had found the key to unparalleled success. He had lost himself in the music, and he had succeeded in getting his musicians to do the same. That being true, he and his orchestra had blended into one and had produced a truly magnificent performance of Beethoven's music.

The Christian attitude is to see Christ at the center of everything. Our goal is to lose ourselves in Christ and his cause in this world. Jesus said, "He that finds his life shall lose it; and he that loses his life for my sake shall find it" (Matt. 10:39). This may seem at first to make no sense at all, but the dedicated Christian knows precisely what it means, and understands perfectly why it works for them so well.

We ought to be able to say as Paul did regarding his perspective on the matter: "I have been crucified with Christ; and it is no longer I that live, but Christ living in me: and that life which I now live in the flesh I live in faith, the faith which is in the Son of God, who loved me, and gave himself up for me" (Gal. 2:20).

Victor Hugo said, "The supreme happiness of life is the conviction that we are loved—loved for ourselves, or rather, loved in spite of ourselves." If this is true, then all of us can take considerable consolation in the fact that God, who knows us through and through, gave his only begotten Son that we might live, and that his sole motive was selfless love for dying sinners, his errant children who have lost their way (John 3:16).

Paul was able to say that he could be content in whatever state he found himself (Phil. 4:11) on account of his way of looking at Christ, of seeing him as the "all in all," not based upon the ever changing conditions and vicissitudes of life. When we, like Paul, see Christ at the center of life, everything else falls into a proper perspective, a magnificent balance. God is good. Life is good. Even death is good, because it finally brings us into the presence of the Christ whom we have adored from afar (Phil. 1:27). Happiness is the inevitable result.

1. Discuss the events of Matthew 17:1-8 in regard to the business of locating and focusing upon life's center. Note especially v. 5b and v. 8. _____

_____

2. Read Colossians 1:17-18 and note how central Jesus Christ is to every aspect of human existence. If I personally do not appreciate his centrality to life, does that in any way change his place in the divine scheme of things? How does it affect my life? How about my future? _____

_____

3. Apply the principle of the story of Arturo Toscanini's rendition of Beethoven's Ninth Symphony to our own service to God. "You are nothing, I am nothing, Christ is everything." Does this provide us with a useful parallel? _____

_____

4. How does the seemingly contradictory statement of Jesus found in Matthew 10:39 work itself out in our lives? _____

_____

5. What are the implications of Galatians 2:20 to the lifestyle and directional choices of the Christian? What is the meaning of the word "crucified" in this passage? How can it be said that "it is no longer I that live"? _____

_____

_____

6. Why was Paul able to say that he was content in every conceivable circumstance? What was his special view of life that made this statement possible? See Philippians 4:10-13. _____

_____

_____

Conduct Your Life in Harmony with God's Will

> **Much of the misery and unhappiness that has been visited upon the human race throughout the ages has come about either directly or indirectly on account of the human tendency to ignore or violate the will of God.**

Karl Marx in his essay *A Criticism of the Hegelian Philosophy of Right* argued that "The first requisite for the happiness of the people is the abolition of religion." In point of fact, precisely the opposite is true. Much of the misery and unhappiness that has been visited upon the human race throughout the ages has come about either directly or indirectly on account of the human tendency to ignore or violate the will of God. Not all of it; we will readily grant that there are some notable exceptions, but much of it certainly has. And, it could be argued that religious people have often done terrible things in the name of God and religion—and even in the name of the Christian religion. But with regard to those instances it ought to be added that, when Christians have behaved badly, they have done so in violation of Christian teachings. They flaunted the teachings of the Bible when they committed atrocities or violated the God-given human rights of others.

Natural calamities, or "acts of God" as they are sometimes called, are open to interpretation. Christian believers will submit that God in the Bible often used such things to visit his wrath upon his recalcitrant and sinful children. Yet in the absence of inspired prophets today to tell us whether or not they are divine visitations, it is probably better not to go beyond what the Bible says about such things. It is therefore safer not to interpret them as divine visitations, since we cannot be certain about them. Unbelievers of course will call all such natural events mere accidents of the natural order. They cannot be convinced that God ever acts in the world either for good or for ill.

On a more practical level, bad behavior often leads to misery and pain. Who can argue with this proposition? All of us know that this is true, and every single one of us can march out a series of examples in our own experience where we have seen the principle at work in the lives of those we have known. We have seen their hapless decisions and their unfortunate mistakes, and we have painfully observed as they suffered because of them. Making the connection between their behavior and their misery is not even debatable. The linkage is as explicit as the natural law that says if you raise the temperature of water to a certain point it begins to boil and if you lower it to another definable point it will freeze. Bad behavior leads to misery and pain.

In our time most people are reluctant to describe bad behavior as "sin," but they will certainly agree that bad behavior leads to inevitable and unfortunate consequences. For example, continual intake of alcoholic beverages in sufficient quantities will lead to the breakdown of certain organs of the human body. All of us know this from a variety of sources, one being our high school health classes. Excessive consumption causes damage to several critical organs: The brain may be affected causing confusion and memory loss. The peripheral nerves may be damaged causing changes in sensation and numbness. The liver's function is to break down the alcohol, but prolonged excess can cause scarring of the liver called cirrhosis. It also may cause disease of the pancreas and inflammation of the stomach. In some patients it may predispose to stomach cancer.

The Bible calls drunkenness a sin and explains that it, like all sin, alienates us from God (1 Cor. 6:9, 10; etc.). People today call it bad behavior, but the result is exactly the same whatever it is called. One will seldom meet a happy patient in a hospital room who has just been informed that his liver is severely damaged. He is not a candidate for a liver transplant because the damage to his liver was caused by excessive alcohol consumption and it is assumed that as soon as he has a new liver he will go back to his excesses. He is going to die and he knows it. It is only a matter of time; and his time is short. His bad behavior brought about this terrible result and he knows that too. Every day that he drank excessively he knew this day might come. He took a calculated risk and lost the bet. Now it is time to pick out a cemetery plot. He is not a happy person!

All bad behavior (or sin) is not exactly like this particular one, in that only some things destroy the body and lead to physical death. But this is illustrative of how every form of sin (or bad behavior) works. It always destroys something. If it does not destroy the body, then it will tear down the character, or alienate cherished human relationships, or demolish the reputation, or weaken essential defense mechanisms, or devastate the sense of self-worth—but in every single case it wrecks our relationship with God. We move farther and farther away from him with every sin we commit. Isaiah said, "Your iniquities have separated between you and your God, and your sins have hid his face from you" (Isa. 59:2). When sin entered the picture man was cast from the Garden of Eden (Gen. 3:22-24). Sin separated man from God. When we are caught up in the practice of sin, we are no longer walking with God, but walking away from him instead.

Irresponsible conduct always has a price, in this world and in the next. And the price is never cheap. The Bible says, "The wages of sin

. . . in every single case it (sin) wrecks our relationship with God.

"When you were born, you cried and the world rejoiced; live your life so that when you die, the world cries and you rejoice."

— Cherokee proverb

is death" (Rom. 6:21). It also says, "Whatsoever a man sows, that shall he also reap" (Gal. 6:7). Most people who live outside the will of God spend their lives hoping somehow in their particular case they will prove to be an exception to the rule, and this will not inevitably follow. They are perennially praying for a crop failure. But that is not the way it works the majority of the time.

The Cherokee Indians are said to have been responsible for this wise saying: "When you were born, you cried and the world rejoiced; live your life so that when you die, the world cries and you rejoice." As Jesus breathed his last, he prayed, "Father, into your hands I commend my spirit," and having said this, his spirit left his body (Luke 23:46). Each one of us is fully aware that we also must someday face this great moment of truth. It can be either a moment of celebration and, as it were, graduation, or it can be something that we dread even to think about. Those who live life in rebellion against God and his will for them live each day with the unhappy consequences of unwise behavior and in the awful shadow of having to face that final moment, of being ushered off into eternity with the nagging doubt that their "scientific" theory of existence is all wrong, and that they might actually have to give an account of their life before their Maker and King.

The point is this: Happiness will always elude us if we ignore God's will for us. His plan is much like an automobile service manual. It is intended to keep the machine functional and operational, to keep it running and rolling. The car will take you where you want to go, all other things being equal, if you follow the directions in that manual. Ignore the warnings, however, and you are headed for a world of hurt. You will be walking instead of riding.

So, if you would be happy, do the best you can to live in conformity with God's will as he has revealed it in the Scriptures. "Keep yourselves in the love of God" (Jude 21). It is the only sure road to happiness.

1. Some have contended that the world would be better off without religion. Communism, which philosophically is virtually synonymous with atheism, has been responsible for over 259 million deaths between 1900 and 1987 (according to the best estimates). Have some so-called "Christians" been responsible for acts of evil? Does this mean that all religion is evil? _____

   _____

2. Is the world better off with religion than without it? Give some examples of the positive influence of religion in the world. _____

   _____

3. "Bad behavior often leads to sickness, misery and pain." Discuss the validity of this proposition. Provide examples to illustrate your answer. _____

   _____

4. Does all bad behavior lead to misery and pain? May all bad behavior be defined as "sin"? What is the modern problem with calling something "sin" or "sinful"? If someone behaves in such a way as to be destructive to himself or others, is that person a "sinner"? _____

   _____

   _____

5. Paul distinguishes between the "works of the flesh" and the "fruit of the Spirit" in Galatians 5:19-24. Are some of these behaviors that he describes deleterious to the body? If they are not hurtful to the body, are they still sin? If they do not do harm to others, are they still sin? What about the charge that "if something does not hurt anyone else, then it is not wrong"? What of the terminology which claims that there are "victimless crimes"? _____

   _____

   _____

6. In 1 Corinthians 6:9-11 Paul describes attitudes and behaviors which, if embraced or practiced, will lead to alienation from God and ultimately being barred from "the kingdom of God." Go through this list and pick out some of the "respectable sins" of our day. What does this tell us about contemporary attitudes toward sin? Are consensus attitudes about any given thing dependable as barometers of right and wrong? _____

   _____

7. Discuss the implications of Galatians 6:7 for the lives of those who think they will be able somehow to escape the consequences of their words, attitudes and actions. _____

   _____

8. Discuss the implications of Romans 6:21 for the eternal future of those who think they will somehow be able to escape the consequences of their words, attitudes and actions. _____

   _____

   _____

9. What kinds of things can you do to keep yourself in the love of God (see Jude 21)? _____

   _____

   _____

Lose Yourself in Service to God and Others

> God does not want his children to view themselves as worthless or useless; to think in those terms we could never be of any value in his service. But neither does he want them to think of themselves as better than others.

Misery is an easy destination to reach. Any of us can get there fairly effortlessly. Someone has said that the recipe for being miserable goes something like this: "Think constantly about yourself; talk incessantly about yourself; use 'I' as often as possible; mirror yourself continually in the opinions of others; listen readily to what other people say about you; and always expect to be appreciated." That is most assuredly a recipe for misery! It is also a general description of egoism.

The Bible places a different perspective on self. Paul remarks, "I say, through the grace that was given me, to every man that is among you, not to think of himself more highly than he ought to think; but to think so as to think soberly, according as God has dealt to each man a measure of faith" (Rom. 12:3). His point is that it is better for us to think of ourselves in realistic terms, keeping everything in proportion to reality. God does not want his children to view themselves as worthless or useless; to think in those terms we could never be of any value in his service. But neither does he want them to think of themselves as better than others. "That no one of you might become arrogant in behalf of one against the other. For who regards you as superior? And what do you have that you did not receive? But if you did receive it, why do you boast as if you had not received it?" (1 Cor. 4:6, 7). Most of our "gifts" and talents are given to us genetically or through an "accident of birth"; in other words, we had absolutely nothing to do with the fact that we are enjoying them. Even if a runner works extremely hard to excel above others in his special area of physical performance, still he must remember that he started out with two working legs. Many others have not been so fortunate. The violinist who practices thousands of hours to reach the top of his discipline must know that he began his life with two fully functional hands. Without them he had no hope at all of being a violinist. Many others have not been so fortunate. He is the beneficiary of rich gifts from God, whether he recognizes it or not. All of us are.

We are all made from the same dust, and to the dust we shall all return. It is good for us to keep this in memory. Too, the talents and abilities we have, one and all, are gifts from God. Therefore, arrogance does not suit any of us. Arrogance, more often than not, is an indication that a person is self absorbed and secretly insecure. Jealousy of others is frequently at the heart of prideful behavior. Thus, out of our envy of the success of others, of their inborn or developed abilities, or of their good fortune, our arrogant actions cover up for hidden insecurities. There is no happiness in any of this. It is just another road to misery.

Alexandr Solzhenitsyn, who suffered utter deprivation at the hands of Soviet oppressors in Russian *gulags*, wrote in his work *The Prison Chronicle*:

> Don't be afraid of misfortune and do not yearn after happiness. It is, after all, all the same. The bitter doesn't last forever, and the sweet never fills the cup to overflowing. It is enough if you don't freeze in the cold and if hunger and thirst don't claw at your sides. If your back isn't broken, if your feet can walk, if both arms work, if both eyes can see, and if both ears can hear, then whom should you envy? And why? Our envy of others devours us most of all. Rub your eyes and purify your heart and prize above all else in the world those who love you and wish you well.

"Narcissism" is a technical term used for egotism. It describes the character trait of self love. The word itself is derived from an ancient Greek myth. Narcissus was a handsome Greek youth who rejected the desperate advances of the nymph Echo. As punishment, he was doomed to fall in love with his own reflection in a pool of water. Unable to consummate his love, Narcissus pined away and changed into the flower that bears his name, the narcissus. This seemingly silly Greek myth, like so many others, contains within it a kernel of important truth.

The more we concentrate our thinking on our own situation, the greater our capacity for unhappiness. Put another way: the less we think about ourselves, and concern ourselves with the well being and happiness of others, the greater our chances of being happy. "That is happiness: to be dissolved into something complete and great," said Willa Cather. The less we think about ourselves and contemplate our own circumstances, the better. As one fellow cynically put it, "You should do something every day to make other people happy, even if it is only to leave them alone." "Those who bring sunshine into the lives of others cannot keep it from themselves" said J. M. Barrie. The happiest people in the world are always those who show concern for others before themselves, who are motivated to help others, and who spend their lives giving of themselves to benefit those who genuinely need their assistance.

George Burns said, "If you were to go around asking people what would make them happier . . . probably not one in a hundred would say a chance to help people. And yet that may bring the most happiness of all. I don't know Dr. Jonas Salk, but after what he has done for us with

NOTES:

The more we concentrate our thinking on our own situation, the greater our capacity for unhappiness.

"I don't know what your destiny will be, but one thing I do know: the only ones among you who will be really happy are those who have sought and found how to serve."

— Albert Schweitzer

his polio vaccine, if he is not happy, he should have that brilliant head of his examined. . . . The point is, it doesn't have to be anything extraordinary. It can be working for a worthy cause, performing a needed service, or just doing something that helps another person." Now this is not an easy route to take, and that is why so many people refuse to go down this road. Stuart Cloete said, "Happiness is a hard thing because it is achieved only by making others happy." We derive joy when we give joy. Many times our lives are joyless because we are not willing to share with others. As Jesus said, "It is more blessed to give than to receive" (Acts 20:35). "We have no more right to consume happiness without producing it than to consume wealth without producing it," wrote Bernard Shaw. When we give of ourselves to benefit and enrich others, we are made the richer in the process. This sounds like a theory that could never work, but in point of fact it is a philosophy of life which has given genuine satisfaction and true happiness to thousands throughout the years of world history.

In truth, the path to genuine happiness is not the road of self-indulgence or of self-absorption, rather it is to be found in losing ourselves in service to God and our fellow men. "I don't know what your destiny will be, but one thing I do know: the only ones among you who will be really happy are those who have sought and found how to serve," said Albert Schweitzer. Schweitzer had himself learned this through hard experience. Already an accomplished organist, theologian and philosopher, he gave up these accomplishments and the prestige that went along with them to study medicine and practice among the poor in Africa. He treated thousands of patients plagued with leprosy and sleeping sickness, as well as many tropical diseases. He impoverished himself in order to maintain the hospital and raise funds for its continuance. He gave himself away in sacrificial service to others. He had truly "sought and found how to serve." Those who have come to know true joy are the ones who follow this simple but magnificent philosophy. Jesus saw his own life as fulfilled in service to others. He said, "The Son of Man came not to be ministered to, but to minister, and to give his life a ransom for many" (Matt. 20:28; Luke 22:27); and, "My meat is to do the will of him that sent me, and to accomplish his work" (John 4:34).

It would be better for all of us if we followed the Lord's example: "For even hereunto were you called: because Christ also suffered for us, leaving us an example, that you should follow his steps" (1 Pet. 2:21). Assuredly we would be much happier people.

Questions

1. Discuss Romans 12:3 in terms of our own gifts and talents. Does God want us to be so humble and self-effacing that we are of no value to ourselves or anyone else? Does God want us to be so self-centered and vain that we fail to realize the good qualities or beneficial talents of others? Is there a happy medium somewhere between these two extremes? How would you characterize it? _____
   _____
   _____

2. What is the difference between a divine gift and a developed talent? Is the line sometimes hard to distinguish between the two? Give some examples of each. Discuss them in the light of 1 Corinthians 4:6, 7. _____
   _____

3. Jealousy is one of the sins of the flesh described by Paul in Galatians 5:21. It has been portrayed as one of the "seven deadly sins," although all sins are in fact deadly. What lies behind jealousy? When we are jealous of others, what is the root cause of this desire to possess what the other person has? What is really going on down deep inside of us? _____
   _____
   _____

4. Is it actually true that the less we think about ourselves and contemplate our own circumstances, and concern ourselves instead with making other people happy, the greater are our chances of feeling fulfilled and content? How would you explain this? _____
   _____

5. Jesus said, "It is more blessed to give than to receive" (Acts 20:35). How is this in fact true? Illustrate the point with some examples in your own life or in that of others. _____
   _____

6. Place the following two scriptures side by side and make the appropriate application of the two: Matthew 20:28 and 1 Peter 2:21. _____
   _____
   _____

7. Read John 13:3-5, 12-17 and make the appropriate application. What is the chief lesson of this passage? Is it really about washing feet? _____
   _____
   _____

Take Pleasure in Simple Things

> "I have learned to seek my happiness by limiting my desires, rather than in attempting to satisfy them."
>
> — John Stuart Mill

Benjamin Franklin observed that, "Human felicity is produced not so much by great pieces of good fortune that seldom happen, as by little advantages that occur every day." One reason that many people are not happy is that they are looking for big slices of happiness, all of a sudden and at one time, huge chunks out of the blue, when every single day little tidbits of happiness are capable of giving them joy beyond measure—if only they could learn to count them as such! In a sense, this is the same as John Stuart Mill's formula: "I have learned to seek my happiness by limiting my desires, rather than in attempting to satisfy them." Simple desires are easily satisfied; extravagant ones are never so. As Solomon put it, "The eye is never satisfied with seeing, nor the ear with hearing" (Eccl. 1:8). If we ever begin to allow the imagination to run wild and free, we will never be able to satisfy all of the outlandish longings that will follow.

Have you ever thought about how pleasurable the simplest things in life are? A clear, cool, refreshing glass of water when you are very thirsty can prove to be an incomparably happy experience. Many times I have thought about how fortunate I am to be able to pour a cold glass of clean water from the refrigerator. Having worked in hot farm fields out far from a ready source of clean water, I can well remember times when I would have given almost anything for a cold glass of clean drinking water. It does not have to be poured from an expensive bottle filled from an exotic artesian spring in France; water from the tap will do just fine when I am thirsty enough!

Sitting down at the table to enjoy your favorite food, as simple and cheap as that may be in most instances, may prove wonderfully pleasurable and even memorable, depending on whom you may be sharing it with. Driving through the mountains and beholding the grandeur of these tall stone pillars that reach to the sky can be a sight that is like no other. Watching a mountain stream make its way through the trees and scrub, the rocks and rills, and washing down to a lovely waterfall, can delight the heart and bring joy to the soul. Seeing a loved one after a long separation is like few other things in life; we will remember such moments for years to come. When I mentioned this on one occasion, a friend came to me afterward and recounted the return of her brother from his service in Viet Nam. He had seen heavy combat and had returned to the family safely after his tour of duty. She told it in rich detail with tears in her eyes after forty years. The feeling of accomplishment that we have when we have finished a difficult assignment also provides us with momentary satisfaction, and, if it is a major project that we have been working on, that feeling may stay with us throughout the years. No doubt each of us, given a few moments to do so, would be able to make a long list of such pleasant things.

What is the lesson in all of this? It is that many of the simplest things in life prove to be the experiences that make life truly pleasurable and in the end make us happy—if we will only take a moment out of our hectic lives to cherish them. I have often thought how wonderful it is that I can go to a local Burger King store and buy a Whopper sandwich (which only costs me a couple of dollars) and afterward bite down into the finest sandwich that has ever been invented by man. Of course, this is a personal opinion. My wife does not agree with me; she has her own favorite. You may also think otherwise. I am given to understand that in Papua, New Guinea their favorite food is sago grub worms. They are consumed either raw and still wriggling or fried. Every region has its own favorites! But the point is that, if we learn to cherish the simple things, things that are readily accessible to us all, then happiness is something that is easily within our grasp.

The more complicated and sophisticated our desires become, the more difficult they are to satisfy. A story is told of a mountaineer who visited the town below and saw his first bunch of bananas. He stood gazing at the beautiful yellow fruit wide-eyed for a moment, until the clerk interrupted, "Want to try one?" "No, I reckon not," said the mountain man, "I've got so many tastes now I can't satisfy, I don't reckon I'll take on one more." There is both wit and wisdom in his approach to life.

I have known many rural Southerners who would tell you in an instant that a hot buttered slice of cornbread and a big bowl of pinto beans are preferable to anyone's brand of caviar. In fact, they would probably turn up their noses at the idea of eating "fish eggs." The same folks would say that a tall glass of sweetened ice tea is preferable to the finest French wine. It is all a matter of taste! Every region has its own favorite foods and beverages that delight the palates of those who live there. Most of them may be enjoyed at nominal cost by the majority of those who make their home in that place. In other words, they are within easy reach of everyone. Almost every one can afford them.

The beauty of this is that you do not have to fly to Paris, or London, or Rome to enjoy any of these simple things. The jetsetters may fly all the way to Switzerland to eat at their favorite restaurant and enjoy the view from a window on the Alps, but you can watch the birds play in

NOTES:

These simple blessings are among God's greatest gifts, his finest treasures, but some of us never stop to realize how absolutely wonderful they are.

_____

_____

_____

_____

_____

_____

_____

_____

_____

_____

_____

_____

_____

_____

_____

_____

_____

"It is neither wealth nor splendor, but tranquility and occupation, which give happiness."

— Thomas Jefferson

_____

_____

the backyard while you feast on home-cooked simple fare and avoid the long flight and the wonderful jet-lag that goes along with it—not to mention the huge price tag!

Norman Vincent Peale put it beautifully in his *Power of the Plus Factor:*

> How long is it since you brought a fresh-cut rose close to your nostrils and smelled that incredible fragrance? How long is it since you went out at night and looked—really looked—at the stars? How long since you listened to the music and magic of poetry read aloud, or to the murmur of the surf on a lonely beach? How long since you tasted homemade bread fresh from the oven? How long since you scuffed your way, ankle deep, through the gold and crimson leaves of autumn? Or smelled the scent of wood smoke? Or heard the wild calling of Canada geese passing across the face of the harvest moon? Too long, probably.

Too long, indeed. Too long for most of us. These are all simple pleasures that far too often we either fail to recognize for the incomparable blessings that they are, or else we fail to take the time and make the effort to experience them, or to savor them anew. They are there all the while for our enjoyment, but we fail to recognize them for the truly magnificent things they are. "Develop an interest in life as you see it; the people, things, literature, music—the world is so rich, simply throbbing with rich treasures, beautiful souls and interesting people. Forget yourself," said Henry Miller.

Solomon reminds us that this is a very important component in the attainment of any sort of contentment in life: "There is nothing better for a man, than that he should eat and drink, and that he should make his soul enjoy good in his labor. This also I saw, that it was from the hand of God" (Eccl. 2:24). These simple blessings are among God's greatest gifts, his finest treasures, but some of us never stop to realize how absolutely wonderful they are.

The same author went on to remark, "He (God) has made every thing beautiful in its time: also he has set eternity in their heart, so that no man can find out the work that God has made from the beginning to the end. I know that there is no good in them, but for a man to rejoice, and to do good in his life. And also that every man should eat and drink, and enjoy the good of all his labor, it is the gift of God" (Eccl. 3:11-13). The wise man tells us that there are many mysteries of this world that we will never figure out. At the same time, though, he hints at another important aspect of the simple things of life, namely that happiness is to be found in doing what you consider to be important work well.

As Solomon further explains, when one enjoys "the good of all his labor," he has come to realize one of God's most precious gifts. "As a remedy against all ills—poverty, sickness, and melancholy—only one thing is absolutely necessary: a liking for work," said Charles Baudelaire.

This is a simple thing also, but understanding it will give added meaning to your life. It is said that Sir Christopher Wren, the brilliant architect of St. Paul's Cathedral in London, which was completed in 1710, on one occasion wandered about the work site encountering the many stone masons as they went about their tasks. As he did so, he asked several of the workers, "What are you doing?" The first workman replied, "I am laying stones." When he asked the same question to a second, the fellow answered, "Earning a living for my wife and children." A third replied, "I am building a cathedral." The last man had captured the big picture of what all of them were doing. Each of them was laying stones, and each as well was making a living for his family, but only the third worker understood that he was engaged in something much bigger than himself, something that was important for the ages. "Cathedral" was part of the familiar vocabulary of Europe. Many of these great edifices had stood tall and proud against the sky for many centuries in a host of Europe's great cities. In his estimation, he was building a monument that would stand for millennia and provide a place for worshipers to gather in the name of God. His work had become his calling; it was more than just a job. He therefore put himself into it wholeheartedly and did it well. There is a lesson to be learned by all of us in this.

Thomas Jefferson was right when he wrote in his 1788 letter to Mrs. A. S. Marks: "It is neither wealth nor splendor, but tranquility and occupation, which give happiness." If you would be happy, therefore, find pleasure in the simple things of life that are available for all of us no matter our financial status. Too, find work that will give you a deep sense of satisfaction and make you feel that you are making a difference. Almost any honorable profession can do that for us if we will only see it in that light. As Confucius said, "Choose a job you love, and you will never have to work a day in your life."

> . . . if we learn to cherish the simple things, things that are readily accessible to us all, then happiness is something that is easily within our grasp.

1. Solomon said, "The eye is never satisfied with seeing, nor the ear with hearing" (Eccl. 1:8). Have you ever longed to go somewhere and finally been able to realize that dream? Afterward, were there other places that you have longed to go and see? Do you think that you will ever stop wanting to go to other places and see other things? _____

_____

2. Do you find it easier to find happiness if you keep your desires limited (note Eccl. 6:7-9)? Is it simpler to satisfy small desires than really big ones? What are some examples of this? _____

_____

3. Make a list of several very simple things that give you great pleasure in life:

   A. _____
   B. _____
   C. _____
   D. _____
   E. _____

4. Read Ecclesiastes 2:24 and then 3:11-13. What is the great lesson that Solomon had learned about life? Are these things that make you happy, or have you failed in the past to notice these simple but satisfying pleasures? Are these the kinds of things that are so "ordinary" that you do not appreciate them for the true blessings they are? If you have ever been away from home for an extended period of time, what kinds of things did you miss the most? _____

_____

5. How important is your work to your happiness (note Eccl. 5:18, 19)? When you have spent a day working, do you feel as if you have expended this time in a worthwhile manner? Do you feel that your work is your "calling" in life? Do you see the work you do daily in terms that matter a great deal, or do you think they matter little? _____

_____

6. The Chinese philosopher Confucius quipped, "Choose a job you love, and you will never have to work a day in your life." Do you find happiness in your work? Do you find fulfillment in your work? If not, should you make a change? _____

_____

_____

Do Not Borrow Trouble From Tomorrow

The times in which we are now living are not unique, but they are certainly different. Someone has described the present age as, "The Age of Anxiety and Aspirin." Of course, whoever said that, said it before the advent of Tylenol or Motrin! Certainly we are living in a time of constant worry over many things. Worry makes for headaches and heartaches and steals away the joy of living. One fellow jokingly said, "It pays to worry. Ninety percent of the things I worry about never happen. Worry keeps them away!" At a shallow level of understanding we appreciate the fact that worrying is foolish, but very often we stubbornly persist in the foolishness of the thing.

Worry breeds pessimism, and the price of pessimism is very high. We pay the price over a period of years, but we must know that the bill for it will eventually come due and payable. It has been said that, "If it weren't for the optimist, the pessimist wouldn't know how happy he isn't." Also, "A pessimist feels bad when he feels good for fear he'll feel worse when he feels better!" A Chinese proverb states, "Man who say it cannot be done should not interrupt man doing it." Pessimism is never the route to happiness.

The history of civilization is not particularly encouraging either to pessimism or to pessimists. They tend either to forget or else ignore the many boondoggles of pessimism. For example, when railroads were introduced in the US, one eloquent authority declared that this would also require the construction of many new insane asylums. He deduced that people would be driven mad with terror at the sight of locomotives rushing across the country. In Germany it was demonstrated that, if trains traveled at the frightful speed of 15 miles per hour, blood would spurt from the traveler's noses and passengers would suffocate when going through tunnels. Joshua Coppersmith was arrested in Boston for trying to sell stock in a new invention called the "telephone." All well-informed people at the time knew that it was quite impossible to transmit the human voice over a wire.

The Michigan banker who convinced Henry Ford's lawyer not to invest in the new motor car company, told him, "The horse is here to stay, but the automobile is only a novelty." In 1899, Charles H. Duell,

> **Pessimists are most often wrong, but few people ever seem to look at their past track record, so they are given some level of credibility in spite of the facts of the case.**

> **"Man who say it cannot be done should not interrupt man doing it."**
>
> **— A Chinese Proverb**

Do not allow anticipation of trouble to steal away the joys of the journey.

director of the US Patent Office is quoted as having said, "Everything that can be invented has been invented." Gary Cooper once predicted, "*Gone with the Wind* is going to be the biggest flop in Hollywood history. I'm just glad it'll be Clark Gable who's falling flat on his face and not me." Robert Millikan, 1923 Nobel Peace Prize winner in Physics, pessimistically said, "There is no likelihood man can ever tap the power of the atom." Hundreds of such quotations could be produced from the annals of human history. Pessimists are very often wrong.

Of course, occasionally they will also be right. Perhaps you have heard of the hypochondriac who had inscribed on her tombstone, "See, I told you I was sick!" Eventually her prediction came true. As of this writing, many prognosticators are telling us that global warming caused by human usage of fossil fuels is destroying our environment and the world will become a hotter and hotter place. I do not know about all of that, but I am not a pessimist, so I am not selling off my winter coats. I needed them this last winter and I predict I will probably need them again next year. Many have forgotten that during the period from the 1940s to the 1970s many scientists predicted with absolute certainty that we were seeing the onset of a new Ice Age. Of course, the new Ice Age never came. Pessimists are most often wrong, but few people ever seem to look at their past track record, so they are given some level of credibility in spite of the facts of the case.

It also needs to be recognized, however, that pessimistic people are not happy people. As they live out their lives, they will likely also be sickly people. Studies show that mental health can influence physical health. And certain personality traits—such as optimism or pessimism—can influence how well we live and even how long we live. Individuals who do not have psychiatric problems but score very high on a personality test "pessimism scale" have a 30 percent increased risk of developing dementia several decades later. The same is true of individuals who score very high on the test's depression scale. The risk is even higher—40 percent more—for individuals who score very high on both anxiety and pessimism scales.

Being an optimist may help reduce your risk of dying from heart disease and other causes. A Dutch study found that people who described themselves as being highly optimistic had lower rates of cardiovascular death and less risk of any cause of death than people who said they were highly pessimistic. The study included more than 900 men and women, aged 65 to 85, who filled out a questionnaire on health, self-respect, morale, optimism, and relationships.

Those who reported high levels of optimism had a 55 percent lower risk of death from all causes and a 23 percent lower risk of cardiovascular death than people who reported high levels of pessimism. The protective effect of being optimistic seemed to offer stronger protection against all-cause death for men than for women. "In conclusion, we found that the trait of optimism was an important long-term determinant of all cause and cardiovascular mortality in elderly subjects, independent of socio-demographic characteristics and cardiovascular risk factors," the study authors wrote. "A predisposition toward optimism seemed to provide a survival benefit in elderly subjects with relatively short life expectancies otherwise," the authors added (*Archives of General Psychiatry*, November 2004).

A study in the August 2002 issue of *Mayo Clinic Proceedings* reports that people who expect misfortune and who only see the darker side of life do not live as long as those with a more optimistic view. Researchers evaluated results from a personality test taken by participants more than thirty years ago and compared them to subsequent mortality rates. They found that people who scored high on optimism had a 50 percent lower risk of premature death than those who scored as "more pessimistic." Besides a lowered risk of early death, researchers found other health benefits related to positive attitude. In the study, optimists reported: (1) Fewer problems with work or other daily activities because of physical or emotional health; (2) Less pain and fewer limitations due to pain; (3) Less interference from physical or emotional problems when engaging in social activities; (4) Increased energy; (5) Feeling more peaceful, happier, and calmer.

The researchers surveyed individuals in 1994 who previously had taken the Minnesota Multiphasic Personality Inventory (MMPI) at Mayo Clinic between 1962 and 1965. The 500-question personality test has an optimism-pessimism scale that grades the "explanatory style" of the participants—how people explain the causes of life's events—and categorizes them as optimists, pessimists, or mixed based on their answers to certain questions. "The results could lead to ways to help pessimistic people change their perceptions and behaviors and thereby improve their health and perhaps lengthen their lives," says Toshihiko Maruta, M.D., a psychiatrist at Mayo Clinic, Rochester, Minn., and lead author of the study. "It confirmed our common-sense belief," says Dr. Maruta. "It tells us that mind and body are linked and that attitude has an impact on the final outcome—death."

Jesus taught his disciples not to worry about the future because the future will take care of itself. The problems of today are sufficient for today. Let tomorrow's problems alone until we actually have to confront them. The Lord said, "Be not therefore anxious for the morrow; for the morrow will be anxious for itself. Sufficient unto the day is the evil thereof" (Matt. 6:34). Most of the terrible things that we contemplate for the future never really happen. They are like frightful ghosts

NOTES:

_____

_____

_____

_____

_____

_____

_____

_____

> . . . people who expect misfortune and who only see the darker side of life do not live as long as those with a more optimistic view.
>
> — Mayo Clinic Proceedings, *August 2002*

_____

_____

_____

_____

_____

_____

_____

_____

_____

of a future that is never to be. They scare us to death in the daylight hours, and visit us in our dreams at night. Someone has wisely observed that: "A coward dies a thousand deaths; a brave man dies but once." In other words, a coward faces death over and over and over again, with every new day he is afraid that it will face him. A brave man, on the other hand, faces death when it is his time to depart. This is not to say that he is not afraid of it; rather, it says that he does not live under its dark shadow every day. The result is that one man lives in fear throughout a lifetime, while another lives in joy every day, refusing to allow the specter of death to rob him of happiness.

In his circuit riding days, Abraham Lincoln and his companions, riding to the next session of court, had crossed several flooded rivers. But the treacherous Fox River was still ahead of them. They said to one another, "If these streams give us so much trouble, how shall we get over the Fox River?" When darkness fell, they stopped for the night at a log tavern, where they joined the Methodist presiding elder of the district, who rode through that country in all kinds of weather and knew all about the Fox River and its perils. They gathered about him and asked about the present state of the river. "Oh, yes," replied the circuit rider. "I know all about the Fox River. I have crossed it often and understand it well. But I have one fixed rule with regard to the Fox River—I never cross it till I reach it." We would do well to learn the lesson that this brave traveler had gained by much experience: Do not allow anticipation of trouble to steal away the joys of the journey. Soon enough we will come to the banks of our own Fox River. There is no logical reason to live in fear of it or anything else before the time comes. Enjoy the journey today, the risks and hazards of tomorrow will attend to themselves.

1. How do we go about borrowing trouble from tomorrow? Is it true that ninety percent of the things we worry about never happen? Can you think of something recently that greatly troubled you – but never actually happened? _____

_____

2. Do you know someone who is a pessimist by nature? Are all of us at least mildly pessimistic? Does it pay to be pessimistic? _____

_____

3. Look up the title Silent Spring by Rachel Carson (published in 1962). Radical environmentalists consider it one of the best nonfiction books of all time. It predicted a spring without birds unless pesticides were banned or radically changed. Needless to say, its doomsday predictions never happened. Have you heard a news story lately that predicted dire consequences unless we make radical changes in the way we live? _____

_____

_____

4. Pessimism is all around us, especially in the news media. The line, "If it bleeds, it leads" is indicative of the content of newspapers, magazines, and now 24-hour cable television. As of this writing, Albert Gore, Jr. (*Earth in the Balance*, 1992) is a modern prophet of doom when it comes to global climate change. His documentary film, *An Inconvenient Truth: The Planetary Emergency of Global Warming and What We Can Do About It*, argues that planetary temperatures are rising due to human causation and that it will get worse in the years ahead unless we radically change our usage of greenhouse gas causing fossil fuels. Do these pessimists and others like them cause you to lose sleep at night? _____

_____

5. Are pessimistic people generally happy? Are optimistic people generally happy? What should this tell us about anything we can do to keep our attitude properly directed? _____

_____

6. Many studies have established that pessimistic people who worry a great deal are generally also very unhealthy. Does this surprise you? What might be some of the factors that enter into this unfortunate result? _____

_____

7. Is worrying a sin? Respond to this question in the light of the words of Jesus recorded in Matthew 6:34. _____

_____

8. What is the best antidote for worry? Respond to this question with reference to Paul's teaching in Philippians 4:6. _____

_____

9. Do you have a "Fox River" story in your own life? Is it indeed best to wait until you get to such a river in order to cross it? _____

_____

Put Yesterday in the Rear View Mirror

> . . . if we just keep on showing up, gathering the strength to somehow stay in the fight, forcing ourselves onto the firing line one more day—then we will be able to work through our weakness and feebleness to the other side.

"We are made wise not by the recollection of our past, but by the responsibility for our future," said George Bernard Shaw. The past can be a ball and chain that we drag around behind us or a proverbial albatross that we wear about our necks throughout life. All of us have done things that we are ashamed of. We have made mistakes, have committed sins, have disappointed those who love us, have broken various rules and been guilty of infractions and transgressions, have embarrassed others and ourselves, and ultimately and most importantly, we have disappointed and displeased our Creator. We wish that we could go back in time and undo them, but that is quite beyond our limited power. What is done is done.

If you deem yourself an exception to this rule, then you are being dishonest with both yourself and God, and have fallen under the spell of your own pride (Rom. 3:23; 1 John 1:8). There is simply no other sensible explanation for your inability to see your own faults in their true light.

Having said all of this, it needs also to be said that God does not want us to wallow in self-hate or self-loathing. The Lord of life and light wants us to change our attitude toward our sins and get on with living our lives in his service: "Wherefore, lift up the hands that hang down, and the palsied knees; and make straight paths for your feet, that that which is lame be not turned out of the way, but rather be healed" (Heb. 12:12, 13). These words were penned to a group of Christians who had deeply disappointed God on many different fronts, who above all things stood precipitously at the edge of the abyss ready to plummet into the nothingness below. What they needed most of all was courage, but that seems to have been in short supply among them. Along with these words of encouragement, the writer urged patience upon them (Heb. 10:36). His point is simple: if we just keep on showing up, gathering the strength to somehow stay in the fight, forcing ourselves onto the firing line one more day—then we will be able to work through our weakness and feebleness to the other side. Half of the victory is just continuing to "show up" one day after another, in spite of all the discouragements that come our way and our own inability to "measure up" to the perfect standard.

There was a little boy visiting his grandparents on their farm. He was given a slingshot to play with out in the woods. He practiced in the woods, but he could seldom ever hit the target. Getting a little discouraged, he headed back for dinner. As he was walking along he saw his Grandmother's pet duck. Just out of impulse, he let the slingshot fly, hit the duck squarely in the head, and killed it dead on the spot. He was shocked and grieved. In a panic, he hid the dead duck in the wood pile, only to see his sister watching! Sally had seen it all, but she said nothing. After lunch the next day Grandma said, "Sally, let's wash the dishes." But Sally said, "Grandma, Johnny told me he wanted to help in the kitchen!" Then she whispered to him, "Remember the duck?" So Johnny did the dishes without a word. Later that day, Grandpa asked if the children wanted to go fishing and Grandma said, "I'm sorry but I need Sally to help make supper." Sally just smiled and said, "Well, that's all right because Johnny told me he wanted to help." She whispered again, "Remember the duck?" So Sally went fishing and Johnny stayed to help with supper. After several days of Johnny doing both his chores and Sally's, he finally could not stand it any longer. He came to his Grandmother and confessed that he had killed the duck. Grandma knelt down, gave him a hug, and said, "Sweetheart, I know. You see, I was standing at the window and saw the whole thing, but because I love you, I forgave you. I was just wondering how long you would let Sally make a slave of you."

Whatever is in your past, whatever you have done, and the Adversary keeps throwing it up in your face (lying, cheating, debt, fear, bad habits, hatred, anger, bitterness, etc.), whatever it is, you need to know that God was standing at the window and he saw the whole thing: "The ways of man are before the eyes of the Lord, and he ponders all of his activities" (Prov. 5:21). He has seen your whole life. He wants you to know that he loves you and that, if you have renounced and confessed the wrong, you are forgiven. God is just wondering how long you will let the Adversary make a slave of you.

Some of us have been guilty of sitting still in the stagnant pool of our own past wrong doings for many years at a time. Apparently we eventually come to derive a certain sick and twisted satisfaction from soaking in putrid self-pity. Others have allowed tragedies that happened years ago to fill them with fear and dread or else with frustration and sadness

NOTES:

_____
_____
_____
_____
_____
_____
_____
_____
_____
_____
_____
_____

What allowed him to be so successful is the fact that he did not permit the terrible mistakes of the past to destroy either the present or the future.

_____
_____
_____
_____
_____

in the present. Either situation is conducive only to depression and despondency. Nothing is accomplished in this sort of pathetic exercise that is either worthwhile or constructive. An old western saying from the horse and buggy days goes like this: "Never holler 'Whoa' in a mud puddle." That is very good advice. We may want it that way, deep down in our heart of hearts, but—make no mistake about it—God does not want it that way. God wants us to move on. Certainly our lives would be better off without the burden of it.

After having condemned his recalcitrant people for their sins and chastened them with the swords and spears of their enemies, the Lord encouraged Israel with effusive words of comfort: "Have you not known? Have you not heard? The everlasting God, the Lord, the Creator of the ends of the earth, does not faint, nor is he weary. There is no searching of his understanding. He gives power to the faint, and to him who has no might he increases strength. Even the youths shall faint and be weary, and the young men shall utterly fall. But they that wait for the Lord shall renew their strength; they shall mount up with wings as eagles; they shall run, and not be weary; they shall walk, and not faint" (Isa. 40:28-31). In fact, this entire section of Isaiah's prophecy is set in motion with words intended to encourage and prepare his people for the next phase of their history: "Comfort, comfort, my people," says your God. "Speak comfortably to Jerusalem; and cry out to her, that her warfare is accomplished, that her iniquity is pardoned, that she has received double for all of her sins" (Isa. 40:1, 2). God was saying that enough is enough. She had borne the punishment for her wrongs, and now it was time to put it behind her. God was saying to her, "Get on with life; make a new start; forget the past." He was not telling her to forget the lessons to be learned from all of it, but was encouraging her not to allow it to crush her spirit or endanger her future. In a somewhat similar circumstance, Paul spoke of "God, who comforts the downcast" (2 Cor. 7:6).

Saul, who became the Apostle Paul, made the tragic mistake of leading the Jewish opposition in persecuting the church during its earliest days. After his conversion, he lived with the ugly memories of the wrongs he had committed against innocent Christians whom he had harassed and imprisoned ("I persecuted this way unto the death, binding and delivering into prisons both men and women," Acts 22:4). It is hard for us to imagine how he must have felt to stand before a congregation and look into the faces of those whose loved ones and friends he had arrested and condemned to beatings, prison, or even death. He had every reason and opportunity to wallow in the past, but he steadfastly resisted that temptation. Instead, he became the most prolific writer among the early Christians and the most successful evangelist of

70 *Searching For Happiness*

the early Christian centuries (in his own words, "I labored more abundantly than they all," 1 Cor. 15:10).

What allowed him to be so successful is the fact that he did not permit the terrible mistakes of the past to destroy either the present or the future. No doubt there were things that incessantly reminded him of his awful history. Surely there were some people who refused to forgive him, and even refused to accept the genuineness of his conversion to Christianity. He did not allow either of these things to deter him from his mission.

He said of his own philosophy of life: "Brethren, I count not myself yet to have laid hold; but one thing I do, *forgetting the things which are behind*, and stretching forward to the things which are before, I press on toward the goal unto the prize of the high calling of God in Christ Jesus" (Phil. 3:13-14). Paul left the past behind him and went on to do great things. All of us have the potential for this as well.

If a person wants to be happy, he must forego the morbidity of holding postmortems. Crying over spilt milk gives life a sour taste. You can ruin a perfectly good today by worrying about yesterday. Forget yesterday! Put it permanently into the rear view mirror.

We must be happy one day at a time. Say with the Psalmist, "This is the day which the Lord has made; we will rejoice and be glad in it" (Ps. 118:24)!

NOTES:

"But they that wait for the Lord shall renew their strength; they shall mount up with wings as eagles; they shall run, and not be weary; they shall walk, and not faint" (Isa. 40:31).

Questions

1. Have you known someone who allowed the past to disturb or even destroy their present? How common is this? Does God want it to be this way? _____
   _____
   _____

2. What is the answer to the problem of permitting past mistakes or sins to interrupt the joy of today? How do we go about fixing this difficulty? What action steps ought to be taken? _____
   _____
   _____

3. Should sin be taken lightly or ignored in our lives? Is saying that we ought to "move on" past our mistakes and transgressions the same as telling people to treat sin as if it was not a genuine evil and did not require repentance, confession and correction? Discuss this issue in the light of 1 John 1:5-10.
   _____
   _____

4. After Israel had been severely punished and had turned from her transgressions, Isaiah urged comfort upon her (Isa. 40:1, 2) and encouraged her to gather her strength for the future challenges God would set before her (Isa. 40:28-31). Is this not what he wishes for all of us once we have come to terms with our wrongdoing and repented? _____
   _____
   _____

5. Discuss the tragedy and the triumph of Saul of Tarsus who became the Apostle Paul. What if Paul had allowed his painful past to crush his spirit and destroy any chance for a major change of direction in his life? Even though Paul may have deserved punishment, would God have wanted him to treat the future in this way in order to somehow "atone" for the evils of his past life? _____
   _____

6. Paul's philosophy regarding such matters is ensconced in his remarks in his letter to the Philippians 3:13-14. How difficult is this lesson to apply to our own past errors and mistakes? _____
   _____
   _____

7. Memorize Psalm 118:24 and say it out loud every morning. Take life one day at a time and deal with the mistakes of today while they are still fresh. Do not allow the mistakes of yesterday or even yesteryear to destroy the happiness that God has made available for you today. Do you think that you can apply this to your own situation? _____
   _____
   _____

Do Not Cherish Grudges

A very wise man once said that "there is no ghost so difficult to exorcise as the ghost of an injury." Truer words were never spoken! Many a heart has been haunted by the ghost of some past wrong, never righted. It is said that Mark Twain spoke of the death of one of his enemies, "I did not attend the funeral, but I sent a nice letter saying that I approved of it."

Ambrose Bierce even defined happiness thus: "An agreeable sensation arising from contemplating the misery of another." He was obviously describing the feeling of satisfaction that grows out of "getting even" with an enemy, or else of seeing an opponent "get his just desserts."

Grudges have an ugly tendency to stay with us, rather like old chewing gum does on the bottom of our shoe. The person who nurses a grudge may have the belief that holding onto resentment will prevent them from ever being taken advantage of again. Ironically, a grudge maintains the illusion of having control while actually making a person more vulnerable.

For example, if a co-worker is giving a special presentation at a staff meeting, one may decide not to attend because of a grudge they hold against this person. As a result, the grudge-holder might end up uninformed about certain crucial decisions made at the meeting, and this may prove detrimental. In the end it might affect the fellow's job performance. Perhaps someone else holds onto a grudge because he wants revenge of some kind for a wrong done to him. Letting go of this grudge appears on the surface to let the other person off the hook far too easily. In reality, revenge is rarely personally satisfying. Holding on to the grudge, and the consuming hatred or burning rage that goes along with it, drains the energy of the one who holds the grudge, not the energy of the person he is angry with. The other fellow goes free! He may not even be aware of any of this. He may be entirely oblivious to the agony of the grudge-holder. Also, grudges have a nasty habit of providing us with excuses for not dealing with our own problems and short-comings. Often, it is easier to find fault with someone else and see them as entirely responsible for the problem, rather than taking an honest look at the role we may have

> Holding on to the grudge, and the consuming hatred or burning rage that goes along with it, drains the energy of the one who holds the grudge, not the energy of the person he is angry with.

> . . . in both cases the innocent sufferer appealed to God on their behalf, evidencing his own forgiveness of his tormentors.

played in the situation. So, in a real sense, it is a way of taking ourselves off the hook and laying all the blame on the other guy.

In one of his parables, Jesus offered the example of a fellow who refused to forgive the debts of another, even though he at first had owed a far greater debt which had been forgiven. The end of the parable presents a painful truth. It is one that we need to learn if we are unwilling to extend forgiveness to those who have sinned against us: "And his Lord was angry, and delivered him to the tormentors, till he should pay all that was due. *So shall also my heavenly Father do to you, if you forgive not every one his brother from your hearts*" (Matt. 18:34-35). Understanding that our own forgiveness may be dependent upon our willingness to extend it to others, we ought to try to forgive as quickly and generously as possible. To fail to do so is to place ourselves in serious jeopardy.

Jesus prayed from the cross for the forgiveness of those who were even then engaged in his murder: "Father, forgive them; for they know not what they do" (Luke 23:34). Likewise, Stephen the first Christian martyr prayed for his murderers as he was dying, "Lord, lay not this sin to their charge" (Acts 7:60). In both of these cases, the sinners involved had not requested forgiveness, nor had they repented of their wrongdoing. They had made no effort toward reformation of their lives and they did not seem to be minded to do so. Yet, in both cases the innocent sufferer appealed to God on their behalf, evidencing his own forgiveness of his tormentors.

These two cases are in the Bible in order to teach us a very significant lesson. In most instances, the wrongdoer will never admit his wrong, let alone attempt any sort of correction or restitution. In addition, that which happens in this world is never the end of any matter. Justice is seldom meted out in the world to the absolute satisfaction of those who have been wronged. On the other hand, God has promised a perfect reckoning of all earthly evils in a Final Judgment which will have eternal consequences: "Avenge not yourselves, beloved, but give place to the wrath of God: for it is written, Vengeance belongs to me; I will recompense, says the Lord" (Rom. 12:19). At the conclusion of his discussion of this point, Paul further explains: "Be not overcome of evil, but overcome evil with good" (12:21).

It is most important that good people not be swept up in the strong emotions and powerful tides of circumstance that attend "an eye for an eye and a tooth for a tooth" type situations, for in the end it is possible for us to be "overcome of evil" and do things that are both unlawful and sinful. The blood feud that took place between the Hatfields and the McCoys on the West Virginia and Kentucky line is a perfect example of how destructive grudges can become. Between January 7, 1865 and 1891 more than a dozen members of the two families were killed, and numerous bounty hunters disappeared, never to be heard from again. Seven Hatfields went to prison, and one was hanged in Pikeville, Kentucky. Mohandas Gandhi said, "An eye for an eye only ends up making the whole world blind." Gandhi was right on this point. It is much better to allow proper authorities to carry out their due processes, and failing that, to permit God to resolve such things in the Final Day.

Therefore, for the sake of the well being and spiritual maturity of the one who has been wronged it is critical for him to forgive others before any sort of desire for revenge blossoms into destructive anger or bitter hatred. Both of these are caustic emotions and having them within us is like having sulfuric acid in a wooden bucket. At first it will hold the dangerous liquid safely within, but as time passes the caustic solution will eat away its container and destroy it. So it is with destructive emotions. We may hold them within ourselves for a time, seemingly without effect, but as time passes they will eat away at us until they eventually destroy us. Have you ever known a happy person who was consumed with anger or hatred? Can you ever remember anyone being happy who was being eaten up inside by a powerful desire for vengeance?

Questions

1. Holding on to grudges is a common problem, even for those who claim to be Christians. Many churches are consumed and even at times destroyed by petty jealousies and the ghosts of past wrongs left unrequited. Discuss this topic in the light of Jesus' parable in Matthew 18:21-35. _____

2. How ought we to address grudges within the church? Is there a divine plan for correction of wrongs between Christians? Discuss this in the light of the Lord's instruction in Matthew 18:7-17. _____

3. Is this an easy problem to fix? Whose problem is it: the grudge holder or the one who is thought to have wronged him or her? Just because it is not simple, does this mean we ought to leave such problems alone without an attempt at reconciliation? What if a serious effort does not work? Has anything been lost in the effort, simply because nothing seems to have been gained? _____

4. What do the words of Jesus on the cross (Luke 23:34) and the first Christian martyr Stephen at his death (Acts 7:60) tell us about forgiving our enemies and those who despitefully use us? Are we justified in holding a grudge against someone else and looking for an opportunity to "get even" with them?

5. Because Jesus and Stephen forgave their tormentors, does that imply that God forgave them? What about the fact that they had not repented of their sins? Explain this personal forgiveness as opposed to God's eternal forgiveness. _____

6. Paul urges us to allow God to right all wrongs and set the record ultimately straight in his own good time and in his own perfect way (Rom. 12:19). Further, he requests that we not permit ourselves to be "overcome by evil" (Rom. 12:21), but instead we are to overcome evil with good. "If your enemy hungers, feed him. If he is thirsty, give him to drink" (Rom. 12:20). Does this sound like God countenances the holding of grudges and the desire to get even with those who we think have wronged us?

7. What about "an eye for an eye, and a tooth for a tooth" justice? Explain the original intention of this Old Testament law along with the Lord's effort toward the correction of abuses associated with it (see Exod. 21:24; Lev. 24: 20; Deut. 19:21; Matt. 5:38-42). _____

Trust in God's Providence

This world is an uncertain place. There are so many variables, so many possibilities, both good and bad. Lightning has been known to strike out of a clear blue sky. Wind storms destroy many homes and businesses every year. Floods erase the wealth of thousands and take away the lives of hundreds. People perish on account of exposure to the elements during times when the temperature drops below zero. Tornadoes and hurricanes wipe out entire regions, killing and maiming, suddenly and without warning. Tsunamis devastate quiet coastal areas, drowning hundreds of thousands in some instances, leaving only death and destruction in their wake. The December 26, 2004 disaster on the Indian Ocean took the lives of 300,000 people in several nations. Volcanoes devastate entire regions, the most destructive having been Mt. Vesuvius in Italy which erupted on August 24 in the year A.D. 79 burying the coastal cities of Pompeii and Herculaneum, and killing untold thousands.

It would be difficult to calculate the yearly loss of life or quantify the waste of precious resources which is reported in the news media every week. Truth be known, it is far worse than is actually reported in the various forms of media, for many dreadful things happen which never appear in the newspapers or on the television news, for little or nothing ever comes to public light about them.

> "I believe in Christianity as I believe that the sun has risen, not only because I see it but because by it I see everything else."
>
> -- C. S. Lewis

These things being true, is there any wonder that so many live their lives in confusion and uncertainty, distrust and worry? Of course, this is a very jaded view of the world. For this picture only looks at one side of life. It sees only the bad things. It ignores the fact that much of what happens in this world is beautiful and good. In fact, *most* of what happens is.

When God created the world, Scripture tells us that he observed each stage of the creative process as it was being made, and declared in every single case that it was "good." At the end of creation, he

_____

_____

_____

_____

_____

_____

_____

_____

_____

_____

_____

Those who walk with God today are assured of the presence and providence of a loving Father who cares profoundly for them and looks after them on a daily basis.

_____

_____

_____

_____

_____

_____

_____

_____

looked at the whole of it and said it was "very good" (Gen. 1:4, 10, 12, 18, 21, 25, 31). Sin came along later, and its dark shadow fell across all of God's handiwork, marking and pocking it with toil and hardship, pain and suffering, sickness, disease, and death. Still, it was not entirely ruined, only marred and defaced. Many lovely and pleasant things remained to be experienced and enjoyed.

Unfortunately for many, in our time faith in God and his providential working in the world have been greatly diminished. In the West faith has come to be viewed as an aspect of our ideological history having little to do with our cultural present. This cannot bode well for people and their general happiness and sense of well-being. Life has lost its intrinsic meaning for them, but that is not all they have lost. C. S. Lewis explained his own faith in the following terms: "I believe in Christianity as I believe that the sun has risen, not only because I see it but because by it I see everything else." Many moderns, having surrendered their faith without a whimper, feel like rats trapped in a maze, without direction and having no solution to the quandary of their lives. They have no answers to their questions regarding ultimate meaning, and because they have given up the one idea (Christianity) that seemed for a time to give them an explanation, they cannot now see anything else that makes any real difference.

Dr. Henry C. Link, the world renowned psychiatrist who wrote *The Return to Religion*, said, "Nearly all of the people past thirty-five years of age who come to me with their problems do so because they have lost their faith. Getting well is generally only a matter of restoring faith." Faith in God gives meaning to life, and our problems are always capable of a solution if we believe that it all actually might mean something and have a purpose. Lacking that, life in this world is no more than "a puzzle wrapped in an enigma."

Ecclesiastes says, "He has made everything beautiful in its time. Also, he has set eternity in their heart, yet so that man cannot find out the work that God has done from the beginning even to the end. I know that there is nothing better for them, than to rejoice, and to do good so long as they live. And also that every man should eat and drink, and enjoy good in all of his labor, for it is the gift of God" (3:11-13). "Eternity" is in every human heart, giving us the sense that as pleasant as some things may be in this world, there is yet another and better country to which the faithful people of God are going, where all of the sickness and sadness of this world has forever disappeared into the reality of the Eternal and Heavenly Kingdom of God. The ever-present human tendency to long for something better and more satisfying, no matter how pleasant our physical circumstances at the time may be, is ample evidence that this world is incapable of supplying us with anything except temporary contentment and limited happiness. If that sense of "eternity" is beaten into submission and silence by the angry protestations of demented infidelity, then the spirit within can only yearn for but can never hope to realize any sort of ultimate satisfaction.

John said in the Apocalypse: "And I heard a great voice out of heaven saying, Behold, the tabernacle of God is with men, and he will dwell with them, and they shall be his people, and God himself shall be with them, and be their God. And God shall wipe away all tears from their eyes; and there shall be no more death, neither sorrow, nor crying, neither shall there be any more pain: for the former things are passed away. And he who sat upon the throne said, 'Behold, I make all things new.' And he said to me, 'Write: for these words are true and faithful.' And he said to me, 'It is done. I am Alpha and Omega, the beginning and the end. I will give to him who is athirst of the fountain of the water of life freely. He who overcomes shall inherit all things; and I will be his God, and he shall be my son'" (Rev. 21:3-7). Therefore, "They desire a better country, that is, a heavenly one. So, God is not ashamed of them, to be called their God; for he has prepared for them a city" (Heb. 11:16). It is within the marrow of our bones to long for a better place, some place more deeply satisfying than the green hills of Tennessee, or the white beaches of Florida, or the crystal rivers of Alaska, or the glorious expanses of Western Canada, or the ocean vistas of Northern California—or anywhere else for that matter—short of heaven itself.

In the meantime, while we yet walk the uncertain roads of life, and experience the frequent vicissitudes of this earthly existence, it is important also to keep in mind that happiness in this world is associated with more than merely the promise of another and better place. Of the patriarch Enoch, the Bible says that he disappeared from off the face of the earth (Gen. 5:21-24), and that he represented more than simply another of those "missing persons" who vanish from our experience every single year and are never seen or heard from again. The author of Hebrews remarks that he "was translated so that he did not see death," but that prior to his miraculous transformation "he had witness borne to him that before his translation he had been well-pleasing to God" (11:5, 6). The Old Testament explains simply that he "walked with God" (Gen. 5:22), even as Noah later did, and was delivered from the great Deluge that wiped out the rest of humanity (Gen. 6:9). Those who walk with God today are assured of the presence and providence of a loving Father who cares profoundly for them and looks after them on a daily basis.

We are never, ever out of the sight or care of God. He is always watching out for us and seeing to our best interests. The shepherd David said, "The Lord is *my shepherd*, I shall not want. . ." (Ps. 23:1ff.).

NOTES:

_____
_____
_____
_____
_____
_____
_____
_____
_____
_____
_____
_____

Faith looks beyond the circumstances of today and sees the promise of a better tomorrow, whether in this world or in the next—and with this promise is soothed, satisfied, becalmed, contented—may we even go so far as to say, *happy*?

_____
_____
_____
_____

His own experience with sheep showed him how God cared for him. He assiduously nurtured them, saw that all of their physical needs were met, guarded them against predation, and lovingly watched over them night and day continually. In doing so, he came to understand that God watched over him with the same loving care and sensitive concern. All of us need to be aware that the Lord sees to our needs and gives attention to the challenges of our existence in exactly the same way.

In another context, the Psalmist put his understanding of this important aspect of our relationship with God in poetic words whose beauty is beyond description:

> Whither shall I go from thy Spirit?
> Or whither shall I flee from thy presence?
> If I ascend up into heaven, thou art there:
> If I make my bed in Sheol, behold, thou art there.
> If I take the wings of the morning,
> And dwell in the uttermost parts of the sea;
> Even there shall thy hand lead me;
> And thy right hand shall hold me.
> If I say, Surely the darkness shall overwhelm me,
> And the light about me shall be night;
> Even the darkness hides not from thee,
> But the night shines as the day:
> The darkness and the light are both alike to thee (Ps. 139:7-12).

Too few of us take seriously the promise that Christ made to his disciples before he ascended to heaven, "And, lo, I am with you always, even to the end of the world (age)" (Matt. 28:20). The Lord provided this steadfast commitment to those who are his disciples for all time, and yet far too many of us flounder in personal confusion and spiritual bewilderment because we do not seize upon this everlasting promise as a hand-hold during perplexing times.

It is said that this promise was particularly important for David Livingston, the missionary whose historic efforts opened up Central Africa to succeeding generations of travelers and preachers. Journeying down the Zambezi River through a country that teemed with dangerous wild animals of every sort, and many savage tribes hostile to his endeavors, he became deeply troubled and greatly afraid. So, Livingston pulled his precious Bible from his baggage and began to read from Matthew 28:20. In his journal that evening (January 14, 1856), he entered the following lines: "Felt much turmoil of spirit in prospect of having all my plans for the welfare of this great region and this teeming population knocked on the head. But I read that Jesus said, 'Lo, I am with you always, even to the end of the world.' It is the word of a gentleman of the most strict and sacred honor, so there's an end of it! I feel quite calm now, thank God!" Like the great African missionary, we need to read the Lord's promise and make it the one solid thing in a shaking and quaking world, and then say with David Livingston, "So, there's an end of it! I feel quite calm now, thank God!"

Nothing is more conducive to continual happiness in this life than absolute trust in the providence and care of God for his faithful children. Paul beautifully expressed it when he wrote: "We know that to them that love God all things work together for good, even to those who are called according to his purpose" (Rom. 8:28). Bad things may happen, but God will always use them for good, just as he did for Joseph ("you meant evil against me; but God meant it for good," Gen. 50:20) when he was taken into Egypt as a slave. If we trust that God is taking care of us, even in the most painful experiences of our lives, we will be able to face it all—even death itself—with a calm and resolute assurance, as Paul himself did: "I have fought a good fight, I have finished my course, I have kept the faith: Henceforth there is laid up for me a crown of righteousness, which the Lord, the righteous judge, shall give me at that day: and not to me only, but to all those also who love his appearing" (2 Tim. 4:7, 8).

Prior to the Lord's departure, he assured his friends that he was leaving them with the most valuable of all commodities. It would sustain them through the agonizing days ahead. He said to them, "My peace I leave with you; my peace I give to you: not as the world gives, give I to you. Let not your heart be troubled, neither let it be afraid" (John 14:27). He was preparing them for his absence with the assurance that his peace would fortify them to deal with the very distressing times that lay ahead of them. Not only would they see Jesus beaten almost beyond recognition and die by crucifixion, but most of these men would die violent deaths on account of their confirmed belief that Jesus was the risen and glorified Lord. They would preach him in a thousand locations hostile to their conviction. While Paul was in prison for his faith, he tapped into this reservoir of spiritual peace, and urged others to do the same. Note that he urged them to "rejoice" at the beginning of these remarks, suggesting that joy is a mental state that may be urged upon the soul of man by apostolic command. "Rejoice in the Lord always: again I will say, Rejoice. . . . In nothing be anxious; but in everything by prayer and supplication with thanksgiving let your requests be made known to God. And the peace of God, which passes all understanding, shall guide your hearts and your thoughts in Christ Jesus" (Phil. 4:4-7).

This is indeed a peace that "passes understanding," for the human mind cannot fully comprehend either its seemingly irrational nature or its surpassing power. It is capable of feats of courage and bravery, of self-sacrifice and dedication, of forgiveness, love and mercy—all

NOTES:

_____

_____

_____

_____

_____

> **Nothing is more conducive to continual happiness in this life than absolute trust in the providence and care of God for his faithful children.**

_____

_____

_____

_____

_____

_____

_____

_____

_____

_____

_____

_____

beyond the capacity of the feeble mind of man to explain. But suffice it to say for our own purposes here, it is fully capable of calming the most disquieted heart and replacing troubled thoughts with joy and peace.

St. Augustine commented, "The ultimate good, is that for the sake of which other things are to be desired, while it is to be desired for its own sake; and, it is that by which the good is finished, so that it becomes complete—all-satisfying. But what is this final blessedness, the ultimate consummation, the unending end? It is peace. Indeed, I say, we are said to be blessed when we have such peace as can be enjoyed in this life; but such blessedness is mere misery compared to that final felicity, which can be described as either peace in eternal life, or eternal life in peace." Faith looks beyond the circumstances of today and sees the promise of a better tomorrow, whether in this world or in the next—and with this promise is soothed, satisfied, becalmed, contented—may we even go so far as to say, *happy?*

Happy people have their roots planted in a deep and abiding faith in God; it is an anchor for the soul that reaches even "within the veil" of heaven itself, a "hope both sure and steadfast" (Heb. 6:9). Thus, even when the stormy winds blow and the shadows of life fall upon them, such folk see Jesus sleeping serenely and unconcerned in the bow of the boat (Mark 4:38), or else standing on the right hand of God (Acts 7:56). God will provide. That is the perpetual assumption of divine providence. We have made a commitment to him, and he has made a commitment to us. If we serve him faithfully, he will take care of us.

Happy people are confident people, and in this case they have every reason to have confidence. Even in the worst of times, they may say with the Apostle Paul, "For which cause I suffer these things: yet I am not ashamed; for I know him whom I have believed, and I am persuaded that he is able to keep that which I have committed unto him against that day" (2 Tim. 1:12). If we know the Lord, and are in a relationship with him, happiness will naturally follow, "Rejoice in the Lord always; and again, I will say, Rejoice" (Phil. 4:4). As we walk daily with God, just as Enoch, Noah, and Paul did, we will be able to rejoice in him constantly.

Questions

1. Many tragic things happen in our world every day. The news media reports some sort of major calamity almost every single week of our lives. Is this really what the world is like? Do the 24-hour cable channels ever report that a quiet Midwestern town is still quiet today? Hardly. Do they report that nearly all of the families who went to bed quietly last night in a small town in Iowa awoke this morning to another rather ordinary day? What does this say about the various media and what does it say about those of us who are consumers of this "news"? _____

   _____

2. At the end of the creative process, God said that all he had made was "very good" (Gen. 1:31). To what degree has the entrance of sin into the world marred the face of his creation? Is there any good at all left? _____

3. "I believe in Christianity as I believe that the sun has risen, not only because I see it but because by it I see everything else," said C. S. Lewis. Does our faith in God and Christ temper our view of everything else? Give some illustrations of this point. _____

   _____

4. Faith in God gives meaning to life, and our own personal problems are capable of a solution if we believe that it all might actually mean something and have a purpose. This is the perspective of a Christian toward life and the problems we sometimes experience. Discuss this idea in the light of some of the following Scriptures: Eph. 1:4-11; 2:10; 3:11; 2 Tim. 1:9; 1 Pet. 1:2, 10; Rev. 13:8. _____

   _____

   _____

5. What lies at the heart of the human tendency to long for a place better than any in this world? Why does this feeling aggravate us even when we live in a fine home in a lovely part of the country? See Ecclesiastes 3:11-13. _____

   _____

6. What are the personal implications of the Shepherd Psalm (23)? If God is my shepherd, what ought this to mean as I deal with problems and struggles in my life? _____

   _____

7. How does the Lord's promise, given to the apostles in Matthew 28:20 an encouragement to us today? Will the Lord truly go with us throughout life? Answer this in the light of Psalm 139:7-12 also. _____

   _____

   _____

8. What are the implications of Jesus sleeping unconcerned in the bow of the boat as the turbulent winds blew and the waves slapped menacingly against the side of the boat (see Mark 4:38)? _____

   _____

   _____

9. Is it really possible for us to have a faith that is both "sure and steadfast" (Heb. 6:9) in the face of all the bad things that the world has to throw at us? _____

   _____

Wait until the Final Chapter Has Been Written

> **Aristotle believed that no life could be deemed as a happy one until it was nearly at its end, or else complete.**

I remember hearing Paul Craft, a country music song writer and publisher tell about his experience in the business. At the time he told the story, he was very successful, having been in the music business for many years. Throughout his career it was an up and down affair, moments of exhilaration punctuating long periods of ho-hum production. One afternoon in 1985 he was in one of Nashville's "watering holes" drowning his sorrows when songwriting legend Harlin Howard came in and joined him. Harlin asked him how he was doing. "Not so good," he replied. "Feeling blue, are you? Well, I have learned that when you get to feeling blue, something really good is about to happen to you," his friend responded. A short while after this, Ray Stevens walked in, and the two of them invited Ray over to their table. After exchanging pleasantries, Ray looked over at Paul and said, "Hey, I just cut one of your songs this morning." He had begun work on his new album, "He Thinks He's Ray Stevens," and cut number two on the record was, "It's Me Again, Margaret." This was a funny tune Paul Craft had written ten years earlier and it had enjoyed only modest success at the time. Needless, to say, Ray Stevens' version of the song turned out to be a *big* success! So, Harlin Howard's prediction was amazingly accurate. When we have a bad day, the sun will probably come up the next morning. When we have had a run of bad luck, something really good may be about to happen. As Yogi Berra is quoted as saying, "It's not over till its over." Until the last chapter has gone to press, there is still hope of a happy ending.

Aristotle (384-322 B.C.) wrote a study of *Ethics* in ten parts. *Ethos* is the Greek word for character, and the difficulties with which this book deals are the problems of character and the conduct of life. In the first part of his treatment of this subject, the great philosopher dealt with happiness. His is an ingenious and important mode of wrestling with the subject. He maintained that no life could be deemed as a happy one until it was nearly at its end, or else complete. In order to illustrate his argument, he referred to the story of Croesus and Solon, as told by the ancient Greek historian, Herodotus. Croesus was King of Lydia, and was one of the richest and most powerful rulers of his day. Solon was one of the wisest men of ancient Greece. Aristotle reports their conversation in the following way:

Solon set out upon his travels, in the course of which he came on a visit to Croesus at Sardis. Croesus received him as his guest, and lodged him in the royal palace, and had his servants conduct him over his treasures, and show him all their greatness and magnificence. And when Solon had seen them all, Croesus said, "Stranger of Athens, I have heard much of your wisdom and of your travels through many lands. I am curious therefore to ask you, whom of all the men that you have seen, you consider the most happy?" This he asked because he thought himself the happiest of mortals: but Solon answered him without flattery: "Tellus, of Athens, sire." Astonished at what he heard, Croesus demanded sharply, "And why do you consider Tellus the happiest of men?" To which the other replied, "First because his country was flourishing in his days, and he himself had sons both beautiful and good, and he lived to see children born to each of them, and these children all grew up; and further because, after a life spent in what our people look upon as comfort his end was glorious. In a battle between the Athenians and their neighbors near Eleusis, he died gallantly upon the field. And the Athenians gave him a public funeral and paid him the highest honors."

Thus, Solon admonished Croesus by the example of Tellus. When he had ended, Croesus asked angrily, "Is my happiness, then, so little to you that you do not even put me on a level with private men?"

"Croesus," replied the other, "I see that you are wonderfully rich and are the lord of many nations, but as for your question, I have no answer to give until I hear that you have closed your life happily. For assuredly he who possesses great store of riches is no nearer happiness than he who has enough for his daily needs. For many of the wealthiest men have not been favored by fortune, and many whose means were moderate have had excellent luck. The wealthy man, it is true, is better able to content his desires, and bear up against sudden calamity. The man of moderate means has less ability to withstand these evils, from which, however, his good luck may keep him clear. If so, he enjoys all these following blessings: he is whole of limb, a stranger to disease, free from misfortune, happy in his children, and comely to look upon. If in addition to all this, he ends his life well, he is truly the man who may rightly be termed happy. Call him, however, until he dies, not happy but fortunate."

Retelling this story of the meeting between Croesus and Solon, Aristotle stresses the point that a life must be completed—finished—before we can truly judge whether or not it has been a happy one. "But must no one be called happy while he still lives?" the philosopher further inquires. He replies that it is possible for an old man to look back across the years and reflect upon his life and conclude that it had been good. In general, however, he reaches the conclusion based upon his analysis of many lives, that no man can really be called happy until he has mostly lived out his life and he is either old or deceased, and then others may safely conclude that his life was a happy one.

NOTES:

Some of us get stuck on one sad and heartbreaking number, like an old scratched vinyl record, and refuse to move the needle to the next song. Life becomes one long, dreary, gloomy chapter that only ends with death.

We would not go to the extreme that Aristotle does in making this point. It is wise to consider what he says in our reflections on happiness, though, for human beings frequently describe others as "happy" or "unhappy" based upon a single page in the book of a long life. Just because something unfortunate or even tragic happens in someone's life, that is not the end of it, and it certainly does not sum up the entirety of a life lived. It may only represent a single page of a very long book. Similarly, a single fortunate occurrence may suddenly change a life of misery into one of joy and celebration. In that case, the days of suffering will be quickly forgotten in the joyful years that follow.

Now, if someone permits a single turbulent event to shape all of the rest of the days they spend on earth, it may very well prove to be the end of the story. In August of 2005 eighty percent of the city of New Orleans was flooded in the aftermath of Hurricane Katrina. Thousands of homes were destroyed; the official number of deceased victims from Louisiana was 1,464; families were uprooted and devastated financially; livelihoods were lost; and many lives were changed forever. Within the city limits of New Orleans proper over half the city's population abandoned their homes and moved elsewhere.

In the wake of the storm some people became perennial victims. Their mentality became that of "flood victim." They were sad and depressed from then until now. Their lives were permanently wrecked. Some gallantly rebuilt their lives and businesses in New Orleans. Others, however, went on to create for themselves new lives and professions in other places. One particular family moved to Kentucky and decided since they had lost everything and had to start all over again anyway, they would begin a new venture. They had never owned a restaurant, but always wanted to. So, they started a restaurant serving Cajun food. The locals quickly developed a taste for their delicious Cajun French cuisine, and the rest is history. They are now very successful restaurateurs. For this family, Hurricane Katrina turned out to be a very fortunate page in the book of their lives. Not to say that this horrible human tragedy was in any sense "good," but it did mark the beginning of a new and more prosperous chapter in their lives.

Some of us get stuck on one sad and heartbreaking number, like an old scratched vinyl record, and refuse to move the needle to the next song. Life becomes one long, dreary, gloomy chapter that only ends with death. Such a life must of course be described as a failure. But it did not have to be that way or end that way. If we had only consciously determined to "turn over a new leaf" and start a new chapter in the book of our life, the whole thing may have ended very differently.

Recounting the narrative of the life of Christ, all four of the Gospel authors close the book on the Savior in a positive light. Not one of them stops with the humiliating crucifixion or the sad burial of his bloody and disfigured body. Matthew closes with Jesus at the top of a mountain with the Eleven and ends with the words, "Lo, I am with you always, even to the end of the world" (28:20). Mark's final portrait is of the glorious Christ "received up into heaven," having "sat down at the right hand of God" while the disciples go forth to preach, "the Lord working with them, and confirming the word by the signs that followed" (16:19, 20). Thus, Mark ends with the Lord exalted, and Jesus still at work in the world and active in the lives of the Apostles. Luke, like Matthew, ends his narrative with Jesus leading his friends "over against Bethany" to the Mount of Olives, where he "lifted up his hands and blessed them," and thus "he parted from them, and was carried up into heaven." Afterward, the disciples "worshipped him, and returned to Jerusalem with great joy; and were continually in the temple, blessing God" (24:50-53). So, at the end of Luke, Jesus is the object of the disciples' worship and adoration, a source of rich blessing to their lives. John concludes his Gospel differently than the others, but his also ends triumphantly. He narrates the conversation between Jesus and Peter, wherein Christ tells Peter to "Feed my sheep," and then explains in shadowy language about Peter's death and John's long life. The final words of the book are incomparable in their beauty and majesty: "There are also many other things which Jesus did, the which if they should be written every one, I suppose that even the world itself would not contain the books that should be written" (21:25).

The point is this: The life of Jesus, in spite of the dark days of the cross, was told in terms of its final chapter. Though for a time he was a "man of sorrows and acquainted with grief" (Isa. 53:3), that was not the end of his story, so not a single one of the evangelists concludes the narrative of his life with the crucifixion. The resurrection and ascension, his seat at the right hand of God, his ongoing work in the lives of his disciples—these are the elements of the Lord's life that all of the four evangelists wanted to be remembered by the generations to follow. They told of his victory over death and his triumph over sin and Satan.

Similarly, Paul's second epistle written to Timothy marks his final composition and a besetting juncture in Christian history. It ends on a note of hope and expectation, and this is very surprising given the environment in which it was penned. Events have spiraled downward since his last letter to the younger preacher, so the atmosphere of the

> . . . a life must be completed— finished—before we can truly judge whether or not it has been a happy one.

second letter is shot through with a sense of foreboding. The perverse and paranoid emperor Nero is on the throne. This evil tyrant has begun his calculated effort at mercilessly exterminating those who have embraced the Christian religion. The wily emperor has been most fortunate in that he has been able to lay his hands on the two chief advocates of Christianity, Peter and Paul. Peter was apparently captured while in Rome and Paul at about the same time was also spirited off to the capital city for trial. Paul was taken into custody in northwest Asia Minor probably in the summer of A.D. 66. In his hurried departure, he left his belongings at Troas (2 Tim. 4:13). Alexander the coppersmith was likely the one who masterminded his arrest (4:14). Eusebius in his history of the church (dated A.D. 325) wrote: "Thus Nero publicly announcing himself as the chief enemy of God, was led on in his fury to slaughter the apostles. Paul is therefore said to have been beheaded at Rome, and Peter to have been crucified under him. And this account is confirmed by the fact, that the names of Peter and Paul still remain in the cemeteries of that city even to this day" (*Ecclesiastical History*, 2:25).

Once already Paul had been "delivered out of the mouth of the lion" (4:17), but he was fully persuaded that events were about to overtake him. He had made his first defense before the Emperor not long before (4:16), and the Lord had stood with him while he courageously proclaimed the message of Christ. He saw himself as already being poured out as a libation, a drink offering, to God (4:6). "The time of my departure is come. I have fought the good fight, I have finished the course, I have kept the faith: henceforth there is laid up for me the crown of righteousness, which the Lord, the righteous judge (as opposed to the wicked judge before whom he was about to stand one more time), shall give to me at that day; and not to me only, but also to all those who have loved his appearing" (4:6-8).

Paul knew that the cold hand of death was shortly to rest upon him. Still, he lived every moment in hope. He went on to say near the close of the letter, "The Lord will deliver me from every evil work, and will save me unto his heavenly kingdom" (4:18). He said that in spite of a clear knowledge that he was about to be executed. For a Roman citizen execution meant beheading. Since Peter was not a citizen, he was crucified. On Paul's final trial he was condemned by resolution of the Senate on the charge of treason against the divine Emperor. John Pollock touchingly tells the story of the final few days of the greatest evangelist who ever lived:

> They marched him out through the walls past the pyramid of Cestius which still stands, on to the Ostian Way *(Via Ostiensis)* toward the sea. Crowds journeying to or from Ostia would recognize an execution squad by the lictors with their *fasces* with rods and axe, and the executioner carrying

On Paul's way to Rome, he must have traveled the Appian way which is shown in this photo.

a sword, which in Nero's reign had replaced the axe; by the escort, and by the manacled criminal, walking stiffly and bandy-legged, ragged and filthy from his prison: but not ashamed or degraded. He was going to a feast, to a triumph, to the crowning day to which he had pressed forward. He who had talked often of God's promise of eternal life in Jesus could not fear; he believed as he had spoken: "All God's promises find their 'yes' in him." No executioner was going to lose him the conscious presence of Jesus; he was not changing his company, only the place where he enjoyed it. Better still, he would see Jesus. Those glimpses—on the Damascus road, in Jerusalem, at Corinth, on that sinking ship; now he was going to see him face to face, to know even as he had been known.

They marched Paul to the third milestone on the Ostian Way, to a little pinewood in a glade, probably a place of tombs, known then as Aquae Salviae or Healing Waters, and now as Tre Fontane where an abbey stands in his honor. He is believed to have been put overnight in a tiny cell, for this was a common place of execution. If Luke was allowed to stay by his window, if Timothy or Mark had reached Rome in time, the sounds of the night vigil would not be of weeping but singing: "as sorrowful yet always rejoicing; as dying and, behold, we live."

At first light the soldiers took Paul to the pillar. The executioner stood ready, stark naked. Soldiers stripped Paul to the waist and tied him, kneeling upright, to the low pillar which left his neck free. Some accounts say the lictors beat him with rods; a beating had been the usual prelude to beheading but in recent years not always inflicted. If they must administer this last, senseless dose of pain to a body so soon to die, "Who shall separate us from the love of Christ? Shall tribulation . . . or sword"

NOTES:

"I reckon that the sufferings of this present time are not worthy to be compared with"—the flash of a sword—"the glory" (*The Apostle: A Life of Paul*, 237-238).

As Aristotle so fittingly said, happiness is more than just a fleeting moment of pleasure or a single page or even a chapter; it is rather to be identified with a complete life, well lived. It is sometimes hard to tell how it will all turn out until the last chapter is in print. Today, among Christians no single individual, outside of Jesus himself, is more revered and admired than the Apostle Paul. He was assuredly the most prolific of all the writers of the New Testament documents, having written thirteen or fourteen of the twenty-seven. Yet in his final days he was treated by the Roman government as a common criminal, cruelly imprisoned, and finally executed. However, even that is not the final chapter of his life. His influence was spread throughout the Greco-Roman world by means of the letters he had written, the churches he had founded, and the evangelists he had trained.

The final chapter of Paul's story is that of the church victorious over pagan Rome. Christianity ultimately became a force to be reckoned with, a movement so prodigious and prolific that even Caesar and Imperial Rome were brought to their knees before its flood-tide. As Tertullian said, "The blood of the martyrs became the seed of the church." Christianity was an epidemic that could not be stayed. Even under threat of death for participation in a *religio illicita*, or "illegal religion," the spread of the virus could not be halted. Men like Peter and Paul, hunted down and persecuted in life, became victors in death, heroes of the faith. Happiness is indeed a complete life, well lived.

The story is never over until the final chapter is written. Each of us is writing our own history daily by the choices we are making. Sometimes it is very hard to detect how it will all turn out. It may look pretty grim at times. But keep on writing. The story is not over. Remember: "All's well that ends well."

> **As Aristotle so fittingly said, happiness is more than just a fleeting moment of pleasure or a single page or even a chapter; it is rather to be identified with a complete life, well lived.**

Questions

1. Does a temporary run of "bad luck" or misfortune cause you to think that your life has been a failure? Do we at times permit momentary setbacks to loom larger than they really are in the larger picture of things? Would it help if, when we are tempted to think in this way, we would take a step back and look at the grander perspective? _____

2. Is there some hidden wisdom in Yogi Berra's quip, "It's not over till its over"? Is the story ever really finished until the final chapter is written? Is this not a good enough reason for us to "keep our chins up" and look for a brighter day tomorrow? This is not our being foolishly optimistic, is it? _____

3. What is the lesson to be learned from Aristotle's report of the conversation between the Greek wise man Solon and Croesus, the king of Lydia? Is momentary "happiness" in the form of wealth, luxury, possessions, fame or accomplishments, to be compared favorably with a life well lived? _____

4. Do you know of someone whose life was changed enormously and for the better by a single fortunate occurrence? Do you know of someone whose life was the envy of others for a time, but who suddenly and without warning met with a single unfortunate event which changed the direction of their life forever? _____

5. Do any of the writers of the four Gospels stop the story of Jesus in the Garden of Gethsemane or at the cross? Why do they go on to tell the story of his victorious resurrection? Why do all four of them end on a positive note? Is there a possible lesson in this for us? Should we allow our own life story to be defined by a single catastrophic defeat or loss? What can we do to keep that from happening? _____

6. Paul in 2 Corinthians 11:23-33 rehearses some of the terrible experiences he went through as an ambassador of Christ. Are these the things that define the life of Paul? Did Paul allow these experiences to make him bitter or hostile toward God or his fellow men? _____

7. The death of Peter and Paul at the hands of the Roman Imperial government was no doubt a terrible blow to the early church. Have Christians allowed these things to define the life of either one of these brave heroes of the faith? Tragedies sometimes happen to very good people, even the very best of people. Will we allow such things to become the defining moments of our lives, or will we wake up the next morning and accept the challenge of a new day? _____

8. "Happiness is a complete life, well lived." What do you think of this analysis of the subject? Do you know of some examples of this principle from your own experience? Would you be willing to share them with the class? _____

Conclusion

> **Jesus was and is concerned about the happiness of human beings.**

Please know that God wants us all to be happy. God wants *you* to be happy. And, he wants us to know how happiness is attained and enjoyed in life. That is why he has laid out so many important and understandable principles which are helpful to us as we make our way in this world. If you follow these steps, happiness will follow. It will take up its abode with you like a familiar friend. Make no mistake about it, though, if you ignore these principles and ideas, happiness will flee from you and remain out of your reach as long as you live.

These things that we have looked at, then, constitute a simple but workable solution to the question, "Where is happiness to be found?" Christ came to bring true happiness into our lives, and thus to share with us abundant life. He started his formal preaching career with a major oration, the Sermon on the Mount, and that discourse began with the words, "Blessed (happy) are the poor in spirit. . . ."

Jesus was and is concerned about the happiness of human beings. In that homily and elsewhere the Lord brought out significant principles which, if understood and applied, will make all of us happier people. It is therefore important for us to do several fundamental things. These are the principal imperatives as we have defined them in the paragraphs above:

We ought to make up our minds to be happy, to make sure that our thoughts are happy and pleasant ones, to count our blessings and be thankful, to act like we are happy people, to concentrate on the solutions rather than upon the problems which so often confront us, to look at life objectively, "as from the outside looking in," to define life's purpose, to locate and focus upon life's center, to keep our lives in harmony with the will of God, to lose ourselves in service to God and our fellow men, and to learn to take profound pleasure in the simple things which so many others tend not to appreciate.

We ought also to refuse to borrow trouble from tomorrow, to forget about yesterday and put it permanently into our life's rear view mirror, to let go of bitterness, grudges, and long-held resentments, to trust in the providence and care of a loving and caring God, and wait for the final chapter of life to be written. It is never really over until we reach the back cover. The best and most exciting things may be just around the next bend in the road.

"Happiness and trouble stand at everyone's gate. Yours is the choice which one you will let in."

Questions

1. What does Solomon's quest for happiness in Ecclesiastes 2:1ff. tell us about our own search for happiness? Would it be difficult for us to imitate his research? What does his final conclusion teach us about looking for happiness in wrong places (see Eccl. 12:13, 14)? _____

_____

2. In the Sermon on the Mount Jesus enumerated some of the important steps in finding happiness (Matt. 5:3-12). What are some of the ones he stressed? _____

3. Discuss the axiom that "happiness is a state of mind that is self-induced" in the light of Matthew 5:10-12 and Acts 5:41. _____

4. Why is it so important to be willing to be happy? Is it possible that some folks simply do not want to be happy? _____

5. Do some people presuppose the worst things happening, and then realize their worst and most pessimistic predictions about the future (cf. Job 3:25)? _____

6. Is gratitude important for the realization of contentedness (cf. Rom. 1:21; Col. 2:7; 3:15; Phil. 4:6)? Is it conceivable that one is not happy because he is not grateful for the many truly wonderful blessings he already has to enjoy? _____

7. "A cheerful heart is a good medicine; but a broken spirit dries up the bones" (Prov. 17:22), said the wise man. Does some sickness and disease have its basis in our general attitude and our unhealthy outlook on life? _____

8. The word "worry" is from an Anglo-Saxon word meaning "to choke" or "strangle." Doubts and fears indeed strangle the joy out of life for many people. How should the Christian deal with such things (see Phil. 4:6-7; Pss. 34:4; 46:1; 50:15; 145:18-20)? _____

_____

_____

9. If every part of the human anatomy has a purpose, what is the purpose of the entirety, that is, what is the purpose of man? Are people happy when they do not see themselves as having a real and valid reason for their personal existence? Answer these questions in the light of Philippians 3:14. _____

    _____

10. Is there a genuine difference between human beings and the lower order of animals in terms of value and worth (cf. Matt. 6:26). _____

    _____

11. Read Matthew 17:1-5. How is Jesus to be viewed in the thinking of the Christian? Add Galatians 2:20 to the discussion. Is he at the center of such a life as is thus described? _____

    _____

12. When Jesus died he said, "Father, into your hands I commend my spirit" (Luke 23:46). Prior to his death, he is quoted as having said, "My meat is to do the will of him that sent me, and to accomplish his work" (John 4:34). This summarized every aspect of his life. What is the lesson of the conduct of his life for us? _____

    _____

13. How would you characterize the ideal perspective on self by the Christian in the light of Romans 12:3 and 1 Corinthians 4:6, 7? Is it possible for us to be too proud? Is it possible for us to be too humble? What would you describe as just right? _____

    _____

14. Jesus did not see himself as having come to earth in order to be waited upon, or served by others; rather, he saw himself as having come here to serve (Matt. 20:28; Luke 22:27). How should our lives reflect this important fact regarding the life of Christ? _____

    _____

15. Reflect upon Ecclesiastes 1:8 and our search for happiness. Is it possible for us to set the standard for happiness so high that we will never really enjoy life? Could it be that learning to enjoy simple things is an important key to being happy (see Eccl. 3:11-13)? Why do so few people understand this un-complicated proposition? _____

    _____

16. Borrowing trouble from tomorrow has robbed many a person of a pleasant today. What did Jesus teach about this (see Matt. 6:34)? _____

    _____

17. Paul said that he had set his heart to forget those things that lay behind him in order to strive toward the goal for the prize of the high calling of God (see Phil. 3:13-14). Crying over spilt milk has given the lives of countless thousands a sour taste. How do we go about putting the past into the past and leaving it there? What action steps can we take in order to make sure it stays where it belongs? _____

    _____

    _____

18. We have the choice of forgiving others of their sins or having our own remembered against us (see Matt. 18:34, 35). When it is couched in those terms does it seem like the right or wise thing to hold a grudge against someone else? _____

_____

19. Belief in the providence of God is the great open secret of happiness for the Christian in the face of the sometimes calamitous events of life in this world. God never, ever abandons his people (see Pss. 23:1; 139:7-12; Matt. 28:20), even when they experience tragedy in their lives. Perhaps it is then that he is the most near and dear to us. So, then, how ought we to show our faith in the face of misfortune? Job's wife suggested one route we might take (Job 2:9, 10), but is this the preferred way? _____

_____

20. In spite of his own prediction that he was already being poured out as an oblation, a drink offering or liquid sacrifice (2 Tim. 4:6), still he saw the prospect of being delivered from every evil thing and eventual enjoyment of God's heavenly kingdom (2 Tim. 4:18). Is an optimistic perspective, even in the face of the worst possible outcome, the Christian view of things? If so, is this not the one that we should aspire always to take? _____

_____

21. What has been the most important lesson that you have learned from this series of studies? _____

_____

_____

www.ingramcontent.com/pod-product-compliance
Lightning Source LLC
Chambersburg PA
CBHW081219020426
42331CB00012B/3052